HORACE: ODES AND EPODES
(English and Latin)

By Horace

Republished Classics 2013

Edited by

Paul Shorey,

Professor in The University Of Chicago

Revised by

Paul Shorey and Gordon J. Laing

Professors in The University Of Chicago

Contents

Q. HORATII FLACCI

CARMINUM

LIBER PRIMUS.

I.

Maecenas atavis edite regibus,
O et praesidium et dulce decus meum,
Sunt quos curriculo pulverem Olympicum
Collegisse iuvat metaque fervidis
Evitata rotis palmaque nobilis 5
Terrarum dominos evehit ad deos;
Hunc, si mobilium turba Quiritium
Certat tergeminis tollere honoribus;
Illum, si proprio condidit horreo,
Quidquid de Libycis verritur areis. 10
Gaudentem patrios findere sarculo
Agros Attalicis condicionibus
Numquam dimoveas, ut trabe Cypria
Myrtoum pavidus nauta secet mare.

Luctantem Icariis fluctibus Africum 15
Mercator metuens otium et oppidi
Laudat rura sui; mox reficit ratis
Quassas, indocilis pauperiem pati.
Est qui nec veteris pocula Massici
Nec partem solido demere de die 20
Spernit, nunc viridi membra sub arbuto
Stratus nunc ad aquae lene caput sacrae.
Multos castra iuvant et lituo tubae
Permixtus sonitus bellaque matribus
Detestata. Manet sub Iove frigido 25
Venator tenerae coniugis immemor,
Seu visast catulis cerva fidelibus,
Seu rupit teretes Marsus aper plagas.
Me doctarum hederae praemia frontium
Dis miscent superis, me gelidum nemus 30
Nympharumque leves cum Satyris chori
Secernunt populo, si neque tibias
Euterpe cohibet nec Polyhymnia
Lesboum refugit tendere barbiton.
Quod si me lyricis vatibus inseris, 35
Sublimi feriam sidera vertice.

II.

Iam satis terris nivis atque dirae
Grandinis misit pater et rubente
Dextera sacras iaculatus arcis
  Terruit urbem,

Terruit gentis, grave ne rediret 5
Saeculum Pyrrhae nova monstra questae,
Omne cum Proteus pecus egit altos
  Visere montis,

Piscium et summa genus haesit ulmo,
Nota quae sedes fuerat columbis, 10
Et superiecto pavidae natarunt
  Aequore dammae.

Vidimus flavum Tiberim retortis
Litore Etrusco violenter undis
Ire deiectum monumenta regis 15
  Templaque Vestae,

Iliae dum se nimium querenti
Iactat ultorem, vagus et sinistra

Labitur ripa Iove non probante uxorius
  amnis. 20

Audiet civis acuisse ferrum,
Quo graves Persae melius perirent,
Audiet pugnas vitio parentum
  Rara iuventus.

Quem vocet divum populus ruentis 25
Imperi rebus? Prece qua fatigent
Virgines sanctae minus audientem
  Carmina Vestam?

Cui dabit partis scelus expiandi
Iuppiter? Tandem venias precamur, 30
Nube candentis umeros amictus,
  Augur Apollo;

Sive tu mavis, Erycina ridens,
Quam Iocus circum volat et Cupido;
Sive neglectum genus et nepotes 35
  Respicis, auctor,

Heu nimis longo satiate ludo,
Quem iuvat clamor galeaeque leves
Acer et Mauri peditis cruentum
  Voltus in hostem; 40

Sive mutata iuvenem figura
Ales in terris imitaris almae
Filius Maiae, patiens vocari
  Caesaris ultor,

Serus in caelum redeas, diuque 45
Laetus intersis populo Quirini,
Neve te nostris vitiis iniquum
  Ocior aura

Tollat; hic magnos potius triumphos,
Hic ames dici pater atque princeps, 50
Neu sinas Medos equitare inultos
  Te duce, Caesar.

III.

Sic te diva potens Cypri,
  Sic fratres Helenae, lucida sidera,

Ventorumque regat pater
  Obstrictis aliis praeter Iapyga,
Navis, quae tibi creditum 5
  Debes Vergilium finibus Atticis,
Reddas incolumem precor
  Et serves animae dimidium meae.
Illi robur et aes triplex
  Circa pectus erat, qui fragilem truci 10
Commisit pelago ratem
  Primus, nec timuit praecipitem Africum
Decertantem Aquilonibus
  Nec tristis Hyadas nec rabiem Noti,
Quo non arbiter Hadriae 15
  Maior, tollere seu ponere volt freta.
Quem mortis timuit gradum,
  Qui siccis oculis monstra natantia,
Qui vidit mare turbidum et
  Infamis scopulos, Acroceraunia? 20
Nequiquam deus abscidit
  Prudens Oceano dissociabili
Terras, si tamen impiae
  Non tangenda rates transiliunt vada.
Audax omnia perpeti 25
  Gens humana ruit per vetitum nefas.
Audax Iapeti genus
  Ignem fraude mala gentibus intulit.
Post ignem aetheria domo
  Subductum macies et nova febrium 30
Terris incubuit cohors,
  Semotique prius tarda necessitas
Leti corripuit gradum.
  Expertus vacuum Daedalus aera
Pennis non homini datis; 35
  Perrupit Acheronta Herculeus labor.
Nil mortalibus arduist;
  Caelum ipsum petimus stultitia, neque
Per nostrum patimur scelus
  Iracunda Iovem ponere fulmina. 40

IV.

Solvitur acris hiems grata vice veris et Favoni,
  Trahuntque siccas machinae carinas,
Ac neque iam stabulis gaudet pecus aut arator igni,
  Nec prata canis albicant pruinis.
Iam Cytherea choros ducit Venus imminente luna, 5
  Iunctaeque Nymphis Gratiae decentes

Alterno terram quatiunt pede, dum gravis Cyclopum
  Volcanus ardens urit officinas.
Nunc decet aut viridi nitidum caput impedire myrto
  Aut flore terrae quem ferunt solutae; 10
Nunc et in umbrosis Fauno decet immolare lucis,
  Seu poscat agna sive malit haedo.
Pallida mors aequo pulsat pede pauperum tabernas
  Regumque turris. O beate Sesti,
Vitae summa brevis spem nos vetat incohare longam. 15
  Iam te premet nox, fabulaeque Manes,
Et domus exilis Plutonia; quo simul mearis,
  Nec regna vini sortiere talis
Nec tenerum Lycidan mirabere, quo calet iuventus
  Nunc omnis et mox virgines tepebunt. 20

V.

Quis multa gracilis te puer in rosa
Perfusus liquidis urget odoribus
  Grato, Pyrrha, sub antro?
    Cui flavam religas comam,

Simplex munditiis? Heu quotiens fidem 5
Mutatosque deos flebit et aspera
  Nigris aequora ventis
    Emirabitur insolens,

Qui nunc te fruitur credulus aurea,
Qui semper vacuam, semper amabilem 10
  Sperat, nescius aurae
    Fallacis. Miseri, quibus

Intentata nites. Me tabula sacer
Votiva paries indicat uvida
  Suspendisse potenti 15
    Vestimenta maris deo.

VI.

Scriberis Vario fortis et hostium
Victor Maeonii carminis alite,
Quam rem cumque ferox navibus aut equis
  Miles te duce gesserit.

Nos, Agrippa, neque haec dicere nec gravem 5
Pelidae stomachum cedere nescii
Nec cursus duplicis per mare Ulixei
   Nec saevam Pelopis domum

Conamur, tenues grandia, dum pudor
Imbellisque lyrae Musa potens vetat 10
Laudes egregii Caesaris et tuas
   Culpa deterere ingeni.

Quis Martem tunica tectum adamantina
Digne scripserit, aut pulvere Troico
Nigrum Merionen, aut ope Palladis 15
   Tydiden superis parem?

Nos convivia, nos proelia virginum
Sectis in iuvenes unguibus acrium
Cantamus vacui, sive quid urimur,
   Non praeter solitum leves. 20

VII.

Laudabunt alii claram Rhodon aut Mytilenen
   Aut Epheson bimarisve Corinthi
Moenia vel Baccho Thebas vel Apolline Delphos
   Insignis aut Thessala Tempe.
Sunt quibus unum opus est intactae Palladis urbem 5
   Carmine perpetuo celebrare et
Undique decerptam fronti praeponere olivam.
   Plurimus in Iunonis honorem
Aptum dicet equis Argos ditisque Mycenas.
   Me nec tam patiens Lacedaemon 10
Nec tam Larisae percussit campus opimae,
   Quam domus Albuneae resonantis
Et praeceps Anio ac Tiburni lucus et uda
   Mobilibus pomaria rivis.
Albus ut obscuro deterget nubila caelo 15
   Saepe Notus neque parturit imbris
Perpetuo, sic tu sapiens finire memento
   Tristitiam vitaeque labores
Molli, Plance, mero, seu te fulgentia signis
   Castra tenent seu densa tenebit 20
Tiburis umbra tui. Teucer Salamina patremque
   Cum fugeret, tamen uda Lyaeo
Tempora populea fertur vinxisse corona,
   Sic tristis adfatus amicos:
'Quo nos cumque feret melior fortuna parente, 25

Ibimus, o socii comitesque!
Nil desperandum Teucro duce et auspice Teucro:
  Certus enim promisit Apollo,
Ambiguam tellure nova Salamina futuram.
  O fortes peioraque passi 30
Mecum saepe viri, nunc vino pellite curas;
  Cras ingens iterabimus aequor.'

VIII.

Lydia, dic, per omnis
  Te deos oro, Sybarin cur properes amando
Perdere; cur apricum
  Oderit campum, patiens pulveris atque solis?
Cur neque militaris 5
  Inter aequalis equitat, Gallica nec lupatis
Temperat ora frenis?
  Cur timet flavum Tiberim tangere? Cur olivum
Sanguine viperino
  Cautius vitat, neque iam livida gestat armis 10
Bracchia, saepe disco,
  Saepe trans finem iaculo nobilis expedito?
Quid latet, ut marinae
  Filium dicunt Thetidis sub lacrimosa Troiae
Funera, ne virilis 15
  Cultus in caedem et Lycias proriperet catervas?

IX.

Vides ut alta stet nive candidum
Soracte, nec iam sustineant onus
  Silvae laborantes, geluque
    Flumina constiterint acuto.

Dissolve frigus ligna super foco 5
Large reponens atque benignius
  Deprome quadrimum Sabina,
    O Thaliarche, merum diota.

Permitte divis cetera; qui simul
Stravere ventos aequore fervido 10
  Deproeliantis, nec cupressi
    Nec veteres agitantur orni.

Quid sit futurum cras, fuge quaerere et
Quem fors dierum cumque dabit lucro
  Adpone, nec dulcis amores 15
    Sperne puer neque tu choreas,

Donec virenti canities abest
Morosa. Nunc et campus et areae
  Lenesque sub noctem susurri
    Composita repetantur hora; 20

Nunc et latentis proditor intimo
Gratus puellae risus ab angulo
  Pignusque dereptum lacertis
    Aut digito male pertinaci.

X.

Mercuri, facunde nepos Atlantis,
Qui feros cultus hominum recentum
Voce formasti catus et decorae
  More palaestrae,

Te canam, magni Iovis et deorum 5
Nuntium curvaeque lyrae parentem,
Callidum quidquid placuit iocoso
  Condere furto.

Te, boves olim nisi reddidisses
Per dolum amotas, puerum minaci 10
Voce dum terret, viduus pharetra
  Risit Apollo.

Quin et Atridas duce te superbos
Ilio dives Priamus relicto
Thessalosque ignis et iniqua Troiae 15
  Castra fefellit.

Tu pias laetis animas reponis
Sedibus virgaque levem coerces
Aurea turbam, superis deorum
  Gratus et imis. 20

XI.

Tu ne quaesieris, scire nefas, quem mihi, quem tibi
Finem di dederint, Leuconoe, nec Babylonios
Temptaris numeros. Ut melius quidquid erit pati,
Seu pluris hiemes seu tribuit Iuppiter ultimam,
Quae nunc oppositis debilitat pumicibus mare 5
Tyrrhenum: sapias, vina liques, et spatio brevi
Spem longam reseces. Dum loquimur, fugerit invida
Aetas: carpe diem, quam minimum credula postero.

XII.

Quem virum aut heroa lyra vel acri
Tibia sumis celebrare, Clio?
Quem deum? Cuius recinet iocosa
  Nomen imago

Aut in umbrosis Heliconis oris, 5
Aut super Pindo gelidove in Haemo?
Unde vocalem temere insecutae
  Orphea silvae,

Arte materna rapidos morantem
Fluminum lapsus celeresque ventos, 10
Blandum et auritas fidibus canoris
  Ducere quercus.

Quid prius dicam solitis parentis
Laudibus, qui res hominum ac deorum,
Qui mare ac terras variisque mundum 15
  Temperat horis?

Unde nil maius generatur ipso,
Nec viget quicquam simile aut secundum:
Proximos illi tamen occupavit
  Pallas honores, 20

Proeliis audax; neque te silebo,
Liber, et saevis inimica virgo
Beluis, nec te, metuende certa
  Phoebe sagitta.

Dicam et Alciden puerosque Ledae, 25
Hunc equis, illum superare pugnis
Nobilem; quorum simul alba nautis
  Stella refulsit,

Defluit saxis agitatus humor,
Concidunt venti fugiuntque nubes, 30
Et minax, quod sic voluere, ponto
  Unda recumbit.

Romulum post hos prius an quietum
Pompili regnum memorem an superbos
Tarquini fascis dubito, an Catonis 35
  Nobile letum.

Regulum et Scauros animaeque magnae
Prodigum Paullum superante Poeno
Gratus insigni referam camena
  Fabriciumque. 40

Hunc, et incomptis Curium capillis
Utilem bello tulit, et Camillum
Saeva paupertas et avitus apto
  Cum lare fundus.

Crescit occulto velut arbor aevo 45
Fama Marcelli; micat inter omnis
Iulium sidus velut inter ignis
  Luna minores.

Gentis humanae pater atque custos,
Orte Saturno, tibi cura magni 50
Caesaris fatis data: tu secundo
  Caesare regnes.

Ille seu Parthos Latio imminentis
Egerit iusto domitos triumpho,
Sive subiectos Orientis orae 55
  Seras et Indos,

Te minor latum reget aequus orbem;
Tu gravi curru quaties Olympum,
Tu parum castis inimica mittes
  Fulmina lucis. 60

XIII.

Cum tu, Lydia, Telephi
  Cervicem roseam, cerea Telephi
Laudas bracchia, vae meum
  Fervens difficili bile tumet iecur.
Tum nec mens mihi nec color 5

Certa sede manet, umor et in genas
Furtim labitur, arguens
   Quam lentis penitus macerer ignibus.
Uror, seu tibi candidos
   Turparunt umeros immodicae mero 10
Rixae, sive puer furens
   Impressit memorem dente labris notam.
Non, si me satis audias,
   Speres perpetuum dulcia barbare
Laedentem oscula, quae Venus 15
   Quinta parte sui nectaris imbuit.
Felices ter et amplius,
   Quos inrupta tenet copula nec malis
Divolsus querimoniis
   Suprema citius solvet amor die. 20

XIV.

O navis, referent in mare te novi
Fluctus! O quid agis? Fortiter occupa
  Portum! Nonne vides ut
    Nudum remigio latus

Et malus celeri saucius Africo 5
Antemnaeque gemant, ac sine funibus
  Vix durare carinae
   Possint imperiosius

Aequor? Non tibi sunt integra lintea,
Non di, quos iterum pressa voces malo. 10
  Quamvis Pontica pinus,
   Silvae filia nobilis,

Iactes et genus et nomen inutile,
Nil pictis timidus navita puppibus
  Fidit. Tu, nisi ventis 15
   Debes ludibrium, cave.

Nuper sollicitum quae mihi taedium,
Nunc desiderium curaque non levis,
 Interfusa nitentis
   Vites aequora Cycladas. 20

XV.

Pastor cum traheret per freta navibus
Idaeis Helenen perfidus hospitam,
Ingrato celeres obruit otio
  Ventos ut caneret fera

Nereus fata: 'Mala ducis avi domum, 5
Quam multo repetet Graecia milite,
Coniurata tuas rumpere nuptias
  Et regnum Priami vetus.

Heu heu, quantus equis, quantus adest viris
Sudor! quanta moves funera Dardanae 10
Genti! Iam galeam Pallas et aegida
  Currusque et rabiem parat.

Nequiquam Veneris praesidio ferox
Pectes caesariem, grataque feminis
Imbelli cithara carmina divides; 15
  Nequiquam thalamo gravis

Hastas et calami spicula Cnosii
Vitabis strepitumque et celerem sequi
Aiacem: tamen, heu, serus adulteros
  Crines pulvere collines. 20

Non Laertiaden, exitium tuae
Genti, non Pylium Nestora respicis?
Urgent impavidi te Salaminius
  Teucer, te Sthenelus, sciens

Pugnae, sive opus est imperitare equis, 25
Non auriga piger. Merionen quoque
Nosces. Ecce furit te reperire atrox
  Tydides, melior patre,

Quem tu, cervus uti vallis in altera
Visum parte lupum graminis immemor 30
Sublimi fugies mollis anhelitu,
  Non hoc pollicitus tuae.

Iracunda diem proferet Ilio
Matronisque Phrygum classis Achillei:
Post certas hiemes uret Achaicus 35
  Ignis Iliacas domos.'

XVI.

O matre pulchra filia pulchrior,
Quem criminosis cumque voles modum
  Pones iambis, sive flamma
    Sive mari libet Hadriano.

Non Dindymene, non adytis quatit 5
Mentem sacerdotum incola Pythius,
  Non Liber aeque, non acuta
    Sic geminant Corybantes aera,

Tristes ut irae, quas neque Noricus
Deterret ensis nec mare naufragum 10
  Nec saevus ignis nec tremendo
    Iuppiter ipse ruens tumultu.

Fertur Prometheus addere principi
Limo coactus particulam undique
  Desectam et insani leonis 15
    Vim stomacho adposuisse nostro.

Irae Thyesten exitio gravi
Stravere et altis urbibus ultimae
  Stetere causae cur perirent
    Funditus imprimeretque muris 20

Hostile aratrum exercitus insolens.
Compesce mentem! Me quoque pectoris
  Temptavit in dulci iuventa
    Fervor et in celeres iambos

Misit furentem; nunc ego mitibus 25
Mutare quaero tristia, dum mihi
  Fias recantatis amica
    Opprobriis animumque reddas.

XVII.

Velox amoenum saepe Lucretilem
Mutat Lycaeo Faunus et igneam
  Defendit aestatem capellis
    Usque meis pluviosque ventos.

Impune tutum per nemus arbutos 5
Quaerunt latentis et thyma deviae
  Olentis uxores mariti,
    Nec viridis metuunt colubras

Nec Martialis haediliae lupos,
Utcumque dulci, Tyndari, fistula 10
  Valles et Usticae cubantis
    Levia personuere saxa.

Di me tuentur, dis pietas mea
Et Musa cordist. Hic tibi copia
  Manabit ad plenum benigno 15
    Ruris honorum opulenta cornu.

Hic in reducta valle Caniculae
Vitabis aestus et fide Teia
  Dices laborantis in uno
    Penelopen vitreamque Circen; 20

Hic innocentis pocula Lesbii
Duces sub umbra, nec Semeleius
  Cum Marte confundet Thyoneus
    Proelia, nec metues protervum

Suspecta Cyrum, ne male dispari 25
Incontinentis iniciat manus
  Et scindat haerentem coronam
    Crinibus immeritamque vestem.

XVIII.

Nullam, Vare, sacra vite prius severis arborem
Circa mite solum Tiburis et moenia Catili.
Siccis omnia nam dura deus proposuit neque
Mordaces aliter diffugiunt sollicitudines.
Quis post vina gravem militiam aut pauperiem crepat? 5
Quis non te potius, Bacche pater, teque, decens Venus?
Ac ne quis modici transiliat munera Liberi,
Centaurea monet cum Lapithis rixa super mero
Debellata, monet Sithoniis non levis Euhius,
Cum fas atque nefas exiguo fine libidinum 10
Discernunt avidi. Non ego te, candide Bassareu,
Invitum quatiam nec variis obsita frondibus
Sub divum rapiam. Saeva tene cum Berecyntio
Cornu tympana, quae subsequitur caecus amor sui,
Et tollens vacuum plus nimio gloria verticem 15
Arcanique fides prodiga, perlucidior vitro.

XIX.

Mater saeva Cupidinum
  Thebanaeque iubet me Semelae puer
Et lasciva Licentia
  Finitis animum reddere amoribus.
Urit me Glycerae nitor, 5
  Splendentis Pario marmore purius;
Urit grata protervitas
  Et voltus nimium lubricus adspici.
In me tota ruens Venus
  Cyprum deseruit, nec patitur Scythas 10
Et versis animosum equis
  Parthum dicere nec quae nihil attinent.
Hic vivum mihi caespitem, hic
  Verbenas, pueri, ponite turaque
Bimi cum patera meri: 15
  Mactata veniet lenior hostia.

XX.

Vile potabis modicis Sabinum
Cantharis, Graeca quod ego ipse testa
Conditum levi, datus in theatro
  Cum tibi plausus,

Care Maecenas eques, ut paterni 5
Fluminis ripae simul et iocosa
Redderet laudes tibi Vaticani
  Montis imago.

Caecubum et prelo domitam Caleno
Tu bibes uvam: mea nec Falernae 10
Temperant vites neque Formiani
  Pocula colles.

XXI.

Dianam tenerae dicite virgines,
Intonsum, pueri, dicite Cynthium
  Latonamque supremo
    Dilectam penitus Iovi.

Vos laetam fluviis et nemorum coma, 5
Quaecumque aut gelido prominet Algido,
  Nigris aut Erymanthi
    Silvis aut viridis Cragi;

Vos Tempe totidem tollite laudibus
Natalemque, mares, Delon Apollinis 10
  Insignemque pharetra
    Fraternaque umerum lyra.

Hic bellum lacrimosum, hic miseram famem
Pestemque a populo et principe Caesare in
  Persas atque Britannos 15
    Vestra motus aget prece.

XXII.

Integer vitae scelerisque purus
Non eget Mauris iaculis neque arcu
Nec venenatis gravida sagittis,
  Fusce, pharetra,

Sive per Syrtis iter aestuosas, 5
Sive facturus per inhospitalem
Caucasum vel quae loca fabulosus
  Lambit Hydaspes.

Namque me silva lupus in Sabina,
Dum meam canto Lalagen et ultra 10
Terminum curis vagor expeditis,
  Fugit inermem,

Quale portentum neque militaris
Daunias latis alit aesculetis
Nec Iubae tellus generat, leonum 15
  Arida nutrix.

Pone me pigris ubi nulla campis
Arbor aestiva recreatur aura,
Quod latus mundi nebulae malusque
  Iuppiter urget; 20

Pone sub curru nimium propinqui
Solis in terra domibus negata:
Dulce ridentem Lalagen amabo,
  Dulce loquentem.

XXIII.

Vitas hinuleo me similis, Chloe,
Quaerenti pavidam montibus aviis
  Matrem non sine vano
    Aurarum et siluae metu.

Nam seu mobilibus veris inhorruit 5
Adventus foliis, seu virides rubum
  Dimovere lacertae,
    Et corde et genibus tremit.

Atqui non ego te tigris ut aspera
Gaetulusve leo frangere persequor: 10
  Tandem desine matrem
    Tempestiva sequi viro.

XXIV.

Quis desiderio sit pudor aut modus
Tam cari capitis? Praecipe lugubris
Cantus, Melpomene, cui liquidam pater
  Vocem cum cithara dedit.

Ergo Quintilium perpetuus sopor 5
Urget! Cui Pudor et Iustitiae soror,
Incorrupta Fides, nudaque Veritas
  Quando ullum inveniet parem?

Multis ille bonis flebilis occidit,
Nulli flebilior quam tibi, Vergili. 10
Tu frustra pius heu non ita creditum
  Poscis Quintilium deos.

Quid? si Threicio blandius Orpheo
Auditam moderere arboribus fidem,
Num vanae redeat sanguis imagini, 15
  Quam virga semel horrida,

Non lenis precibus fata recludere,
Nigro compulerit Mercurius gregi?
Durum: sed levius fit patientia,
  Quidquid corrigerest nefas. 20

XXV.

Parcius iunctas quatiunt fenestras
Iactibus crebris iuvenes protervi,
Nec tibi somnos adimunt, amatque
  Ianua limen,

Quae prius multum facilis movebat 5
Cardines. Audis minus et minus iam:
'Me tuo longas pereunte noctes,
  Lydia, dormis?'

Invicem moechos anus arrogantis
Flebis in solo levis angiportu, 10
Thracio bacchante magis sub inter-
  lunia vento,

Cum tibi flagrans amor et libido,
Quae solet matres furiare equorum,
Saeviet circa iecur ulcerosum, 15
  Non sine questu,

Laeta quod pubes hedera virenti
Gaudeat pulla magis atque myrto,
Aridas frondes hiemis sodali
  Dedicet Hebro. 20

XXVI.

Musis amicus tristitiam et metus
Tradam protervis in mare Creticum
  Portare ventis, quis sub Arcto
    Rex gelidae metuatur orae,

Quid Tiridaten terreat, unice 5
Securus. O quae fontibus integris
  Gaudes, apricos necte flores,
    Necte meo Lamiae coronam,

Pimplei dulcis. Nil sine te mei
Prosunt honores: hunc fidibus novis, 10
  Hunc Lesbio sacrare plectro
    Teque tuasque decet sorores.

XXVII.

Natis in usum laetitiae scyphis
Pugnare Thracumst: tollite barbarum
  Morem, verecundumque Bacchum
    Sanguineis prohibete rixis.

Vino et lucernis Medus acinaces 5
Immane quantum discrepat: impium
  Lenite clamorem, sodales,
    Et cubito remanete presso.

Voltis severi me quoque sumere
Partem Falerni? Dicat Opuntiae 10
  Frater Megillae quo beatus
    Volnere, qua pereat sagitta.

Cessat voluntas? Non alia bibam
Mercede. Quae te cumque domat Venus,
  Non erubescendis adurit 15
    Ignibus ingenuoque semper

Amore peccas. Quidquid habes, age,
Depone tutis auribus. A miser,
  Quanta laborabas Charybdi,
    Digne puer meliore flamma! 20

Quae saga, quis te solvere Thessalis
Magus venenis, quis poterit deus?
  Vix inligatum te triformi
    Pegasus expediet Chimaera.

XXVIII.

Te maris et terrae numeroque carentis arenae
  Mensorem cohibent, Archyta,
Pulveris exigui prope litus parva Matinum
  Munera, nec quicquam tibi prodest
Aerias temptasse domos animoque rotundum 5
  Percurrisse polum morituro.
Occidit et Pelopis genitor, conviva deorum,
  Tithonusque remotus in auras
Et Iovis arcanis Minos admissus, habentque
  Tartara Panthoiden iterum Orco 10
Demissum, quamvis clipeo Troiana refixo
  Tempora testatus nihil ultra

Nervos atque cutem morti concesserat atrae,
  Iudice te non sordidus auctor
Naturae verique. Sed omnes una manet nox 15
  Et calcanda semel via leti.
Dant alios Furiae torvo spectacula Marti,
  Exitiost avidum mare nautis;
Mixta senum ac iuvenum densentur funera; nullum
  Saeva caput Proserpina fugit: 20
Me quoque devexi rapidus comes Orionis
  Illyricis Notus obruit undis.
At tu, nauta, vagae ne parce malignus arenae
  Ossibus et capiti inhumato
Particulam dare: sic, quodcumque minabitur Eurus 25
  Fluctibus Hesperiis, Venusinae
Plectantur silvae te sospite, multaque merces,
  Unde potest, tibi defluat aequo
Ab Iove Neptunoque sacri custode Tarenti.
  Neglegis immeritis nocituram 30
Postmodo te natis fraudem committere? Fors et
  Debita iura vicesque superbae
Te maneant ipsum: precibus non linquar inultis,
  Teque piacula nulla resolvent.
Quamquam festinas, non est mora longa; licebit 35
  Iniecto ter pulvere curras.

XXIX.

Icci, beatis nunc Arabum invides
Gazis et acrem militiam paras
  Non ante devictis Sabaeae
    Regibus, horribilique Medo

Nectis catenas? Quae tibi virginum 5
Sponso necato barbara serviet?
  Puer quis ex aula capillis
    Ad cyathum statuetur unctis,

Doctus sagittas tendere Sericas
Arcu paterno? Quis neget arduis 10
  Pronos relabi posse rivos
    Montibus et Tiberim reverti,

Cum tu coemptos undique nobilis
Libros Panaeti Socraticam et domum
  Mutare loricis Hiberis, 15
    Pollicitus meliora, tendis ?

XXX.

O Venus, regina Cnidi Paphique,
Sperne dilectam Cypron et vocantis
Ture te multo Glycerae decoram
    Transfer in aedem.

Fervidus tecum puer et solutis 5
Gratiae zonis properentque Nymphae
Et parum comis sine te Iuventas
    Mercuriusque.

XXXI.

Quid dedicatum poscit Apollinem
Vates? Quid orat, de patera novum
  Fundens liquorem? Non opimae
    Sardiniae segetes feracis,

Non aestuosae grata Calabriae 5
Armenta, non aurum aut ebur Indicum,
  Non rura, quae Liris quieta
    Mordet aqua taciturnus amnis.

Premant Calena falce quibus dedit
Fortuna vitem, dives et aureis 10
  Mercator exsiccet culullis
    Vina Syra reparata merce,

Dis carus ipsis, quippe ter et quater
Anno revisens aequor Atlanticum
  Impune. Me pascunt olivae, 15
    Me cichorea levesque malvae.

Frui paratis et valido mihi,
Latoe, dones et precor integra
  Cum mente nec turpem senectam
    Degere nec cithara carentem. 20

XXXII.

Poscimur. Siquid vacui sub umbra
Lusimus tecum, quod et hunc in annum

Vivat et pluris, age dic Latinum,
  Barbite, carmen,

Lesbio primum modulate civi, 5
Qui ferox bello tamen inter arma,
Sive iactatam religarat udo
  Litore navim,

Liberum et Musas Veneremque et illi
Semper haerentem puerum canebat, 10
Et Lycum nigris oculis nigroque
  Crine decorum.

O decus Phoebi et dapibus supremi
Grata testudo Iovis, o laborum
Dulce lenimen, mihi cumque salve 15
  Rite vocanti!

XXXIII.

Albi, ne doleas plus nimio memor
Immitis Glycerae, neu miserabilis
Decantes elegos, cur tibi iunior
  Laesa praeniteat fide.

Insignem tenui fronte Lycorida 5
Cyri torret amor, Cyrus in asperam
Declinat Pholoen; sed prius Apulis
  Iungentur capreae lupis

Quam turpi Pholoe peccet adultero.
Sic visum Veneri, cui placet impares 10
Formas atque animos sub iuga aenea
  Saevo mittere cum ioco.

Ipsum me melior cum peteret Venus,
Grata detinuit compede Myrtale
Libertina, fretis acrior Hadriae 15
  Curvantis Calabros sinus.

XXXIV.

Parcus deorum cultor et infrequens,
Insanientis dum sapientiae

Consultus erro, nunc retrorsum
   Vela dare atque iterare cursus

Cogor relictos. Namque Diespiter, 5
Igni corusco nubila dividens
   Plerumque, per purum tonantis
    Egit equos volucremque currum,

Quo bruta tellus et vaga flumina,
Quo Styx et invisi horrida Taenari 10
   Sedes Atlanteusque finis
    Concutitur. Valet ima summis

Mutare et insignem attenuat deus,
Obscura promens; hinc apicem rapax
   Fortuna cum stridore acuto 15
    Sustulit, hic posuisse gaudet.

XXXV.

O diva, gratum quae regis Antium,
Praesens vel imo tollere de gradu
   Mortale corpus vel superbos
    Vertere funeribus triumphos,

Te pauper ambit sollicita prece 5
Ruris colonus, te dominam aequoris
   Quicumque Bithyna lacessit
    Carpathium pelagus carina.

Te Dacus asper, te profugi Scythae
Urbesque gentesque et Latium ferox 10
   Regumque matres barbarorum et
    Purpurei metuunt tyranni,

Iniurioso ne pede proruas
Stantem columnam, neu populus frequens
   Ad arma cessantis, ad arma 15
    Concitet imperiumque frangat.

Te semper anteit saeva Necessitas,
Clavos trabalis et cuneos manu
   Gestans aena, nec severus
    Uncus abest liquidumque plumbum. 20

Te Spes et albo rara Fides colit
Velata panno, nec comitem abnegat,

Utcumque mutata potentis
  Veste domos inimica linquis.

At volgus infidum et meretrix retro 25
Periura cedit, diffugiunt cadis
  Cum faece siccatis amici
    Ferre iugum pariter dolosi.

Serves iturum Caesarem in ultimos
Orbis Britannos et iuvenum recens 30
  Examen Eois timendum
    Partibus Oceanoque rubro.

Eheu cicatricum et sceleris pudet
Fratrumque. Quid nos dura refugimus
  Aetas? quid intactum nefasti
    Liquimus? unde manum iuventus 35

Metu deorum continuit? quibus
Pepercit aris? O utinam nova
  Incude diffingas retusum in
    Massagetas Arabasque ferrum! 40

XXXVI.

Et ture et fidibus iuvat
  Placare et vituli sanguine debito
Custodes Numidae deos,
  Qui nunc Hesperia sospes ab ultima
Caris multa sodalibus, 5
  Nulli plura tamen dividit oscula
Quam dulci Lamiae, memor
  Actae non alio rege puertiae
Mutataeque simul togae.
  Cressa ne careat pulchra dies nota, 10
Neu promptae modus amphorae
  Neu morem in Salium sit requies pedum,
Neu multi Damalis meri
  Bassum Threicia vincat amystide,
Neu desint epulis rosae 15
  Neu vivax apium neu breve lilium.
Omnes in Damalin putris
  Deponent oculos, nec Damalis novo
Divelletur adultero,
  Lascivis hederis ambitiosior. 20

XXXVII.

Nunc est bibendum, nunc pede libero
Pulsanda tellus, nunc Saliaribus
  Ornare pulvinar deorum
    Tempus erat dapibus, sodales.

Antehac nefas depromere Caecubum 5
Cellis avitis, dum Capitolio
  Regina dementis ruinas
    Funus et imperio parabat

Contaminato cum grege turpium
Morbo virorum, quidlibet impotens 10
  Sperare fortunaque dulci
    Ebria. Sed minuit furorem

Vix una sospes navis ab ignibus,
Mentemque lymphatam Mareotico
  Redegit in veros timores 15
    Caesar, ab Italia volantem

Remis adurgens, accipiter velut
Mollis columbas aut leporem citus
  Venator in campis nivalis
    Haemoniae, daret ut catenis 20

Fatale monstrum. Quae generosius
Perire quaerens nec muliebriter
  Expavit ensem nec latentis
    Classe cita reparavit oras.

Ausa et iacentem visere regiam 25
Voltu sereno, fortis et asperas
  Tractare serpentes, ut atrum
    Corpore combiberet venenum,

Deliberata morte ferocior,
Saevis Liburnis scilicet invidens 30
  Privata deduci superbo
    Non humilis mulier triumpho.

XXXVIII.

Persicos odi, puer, apparatus;
Displicent nexae philyra coronae;

Mitte sectari, rosa quo locorum
  Sera moretur.

Simplici myrto nihil adlabores 5
Sedulus curo: neque te ministrum
Dedecet myrtus neque me sub arta
  Vite bibentem.

CARMINUM

LIBER SECUNDUS.

I.

Motum ex Metello consule civicum
Bellique causas et vitia et modos
  Ludumque Fortunae gravisque
    Principum amicitias et arma

Nondum expiatis uncta cruoribus, 5
Periculosae plenum opus aleae,
  Tractas et incedis per ignis
    Suppositos cineri doloso.

Paullum severae Musa tragoediae
Desit theatris; mox ubi publicas 10
  Res ordinaris, grande munus
    Cecropio repetes cothurno,

Insigne maestis praesidium reis
Et consulenti, Pollio, Curiae,
  Cui laurus aeternos honores 15
    Delmatico peperit triumpho.

Iam nunc minaci murmure cornuum
Perstringis auris, iam litui strepunt,
  Iam fulgor armorum fugacis
    Terret equos equitumque voltus. 20

Audire magnos iam videor duces,
Non indecoro pulvere sordidos,
  Et cuncta terrarum subacta
    Praeter atrocem animum Catonis.

Iuno et deorum quisquis amicior 25
Afris inulta cesserat impotens
  Tellure victorum nepotes
    Rettulit inferias Iugurthae.

Quis non Latino sanguine pinguior
Campus sepulcris impia proelia 30
  Testatur auditumque Medis
    Hesperiae sonitum ruinae?

Qui gurges aut quae flumina lugubris
Ignara belli? quod mare Dauniae
  Non decoloravere caedes? 35
    Quae caret ora cruore nostro?

Sed ne relictis, Musa procax, iocis
Ceae retractes munera neniae,
  Mecum Dionaeo sub antro
    Quaere modos leviore plectro.

II.

Nullus argento color est avaris
Abdito terris, inimice lamnae
Crispe Sallusti, nisi temperato
  Splendeat usu.

Vivet extento Proculeius aevo, 5
Notus in fratres animi paterni;
Illum aget penna metuente solvi
  Fama superstes.

Latius regnes avidum domando
Spiritum, quam si Libyam remotis 10
Gadibus iungas et uterque Poenus
  Serviat uni.

Crescit indulgens sibi dirus hydrops
Nec sitim pellit, nisi causa morbi
Fugerit venis et aquosus albo 15
  Corpore languor.

Redditum Cyri solio Phraaten
Dissidens plebi numero beatorum
Eximit Virtus populumque falsis
  Dedocet uti 20

Vocibus, regnum et diadema tutum
Deferens uni propriamque laurum,
Quisquis ingentis oculo inretorto
  Spectat acervos.

III.

Aequam memento rebus in arduis
Servare mentem, non secus in bonis
  Ab insolenti temperatam
    Laetitia, moriture Delli,

Seu maestus omni tempore vixeris, 5
Seu te in remoto gramine per dies
  Festos reclinatum bearis
    Interiore nota Falerni.

Quo pinus ingens albaque populus
Umbram hospitalem consociare amant 10
  Ramis? Quid obliquo laborat
    Lympha fugax trepidare rivo?

Huc vina et unguenta et nimium brevis
Flores amoenae ferre iube rosae,
  Dum res et aetas et sororum
    Fila trium patiuntur atra. 15

Cedes coemptis saltibus et domo
Villaque, flavus quam Tiberis lavit,
  Cedes, et exstructis in altum
    Divitiis potietur heres.

Divesne prisco natus ab Inacho 20
Nil interest an pauper et infima
  De gente sub divo moreris,
    Victima nil miserantis Orci.

Omnes eodem cogimur, omnium
Versatur urna serius ocius 25
  Sors exitura et nos in aeternum
    Exsilium impositura cumbae.

IV.

Ne sit ancillae tibi amor pudori,
Xanthia Phoceu! Prius insolentem
Serva Briseis niveo colore
   Movit Achillem;

Movit Aiacem Telamone natum 5
Forma captivae dominum Tecmessae;
Arsit Atrides medio in triumpho
   Virgine rapta,

Barbarae postquam cecidere turmae
Thessalo victore et ademptus Hector 10
Tradidit fessis leviora tolli
   Pergama Grais.

Nescias an te generum beati
Phyllidis flavae decorent parentes;
Regium certe genus et penatis 15
   Maeret iniquos.

Crede non illam tibi de scelesta
Plebe dilectam, neque sic fidelem,
Sic lucro aversam potuisse nasci
   Matre pudenda. 20

Bracchia et voltum teretesque suras
Integer laudo; fuge suspicari,
Cuius octavum trepidavit aetas
   Claudere lustrum.

V.

Nondum subacta ferre iugum valet
Cervice, nondum munia comparis
   Aequare nec tauri ruentis
     In venerem tolerare pondus.

Circa virentis est animus tuae 5
Campos iuvencae, nunc fluviis gravem
   Solantis aestum, nunc in udo
     Ludere cum vitulis salicto

Praegestientis. Tolle cupidinem
Immitis uvae: iam tibi lividos 10
   Distinguet autumnus racemos
     Purpureo varius colore.

Iam te sequetur: currit enim ferox
Aetas, et illi, quos tibi dempserit,
  Adponet annos; iam proterva 15
    Fronte petet Lalage maritum,

Dilecta quantum non Pholoe fugax,
Non Chloris, albo sic umero nitens
  Ut pura nocturno renidet
    Luna mari, Cnidiusve Gyges, 20

Quem si puellarum insereres choro,
Mire sagacis falleret hospites
  Discrimen obscurum solutis
    Crinibus ambiguoque voltu.

VI.

Septimi, Gadis aditure mecum et
Cantabrum indoctum iuga ferre nostra et
Barbaras Syrtis, ubi Maura semper
  Aestuat unda:

Tibur Argeo positum colono 5
Sit meae sedes utinam senectae,
Sit modus lasso maris et viarum
  Militiaeque.

Unde si Parcae prohibent iniquae,
Dulce pellitis ovibus Galaesi 10
Flumen et regnata petam Laconi
  Rura Phalantho.

Ille terrarum mihi praeter omnis
Angulus ridet, ubi non Hymetto
Mella decedunt viridique certat 15
  Baca Venafro;

Ver ubi longum tepidasque praebet
Iuppiter brumas, et amicus Aulon
Fertili Baccho minimum Falernis
  Invidet uvis. 20

Ille te mecum locus et beatae
Postulant arces; ibi tu calentem
Debita sparges lacrima favillam
  Vatis amici.

VII.

O saepe mecum tempus in ultimum
Deducte Bruto militiae duce,
  Quis te redonavit Quiritem
    Dis patriis Italoque caelo,

Pompei, meorum prime sodalium, 5
Cum quo morantem saepe diem mero
  Fregi, coronatus nitentis
    Malobathro Syrio capillos?

Tecum Philippos et celerem fugam
Sensi relicta non bene parmula, 10
  Cum fracta virtus et minaces
    Turpe solum tetigere mento.

Sed me per hostis Mercurius celer
Denso paventem sustulit aere;
  Te rursus in bellum resorbens 15
    Unda fretis tulit aestuosis.

Ergo obligatam redde Iovi dapem,
Longaque fessum militia latus
  Depone sub lauru mea nec
    Parce cadis tibi destinatis. 20

Oblivioso levia Massico
Ciboria exple, funde capacibus
  Unguenta de conchis. Quis udo
    Deproperare apio coronas

Curatve myrto? Quem Venus arbitrum 25
Dicet bibendi? Non ego sanius
  Bacchabor Edonis: recepto
    Dulce mihi furerest amico.

VIII.

Ulla si iuris tibi peierati
Poena, Barine, nocuisset umquam,
Dente si nigro fieres vel uno
  Turpior ungui,

Crederem. Sed tu simul obligasti 5
Perfidum votis caput, enitescis

Pulchrior multo, iuvenumque prodis
  Publica cura.

Expedit matris cineres opertos
Fallere et toto taciturna noctis 10
Signa cum caelo gelidaque divos
  Morte carentis.

Ridet hoc, inquam, Venus ipsa, rident
Simplices Nymphae ferus et Cupido,
Semper ardentis acuens sagittas 15
  Cote cruenta.

Adde quod pubes tibi crescit omnis,
Servitus crescit nova, nec priores
Impiae tectum dominae relinquunt,
  Saepe minati. 20

Te suis matres motuunt iuvencis,
Te senes parci miseraeque nuper
Virgines nuptae, tua ne retardet
  Aura maritos.

IX.

Non semper imbres nubibus hispidos
Manant in agros aut mare Caspium
  Vexant inaequales procellae
    Usque, nec Armeniis in oris,

Amice Valgi, stat glacies iners 5
Mensis per omnis, aut Aquilonibus
  Querceta Gargani laborant
    Et foliis viduantur orni:

Tu semper urges flebilibus modis
Mysten ademptum, nec tibi Vespero 10
  Surgente decedunt amores
    Nec rapidum fugiente solem.

At non ter aevo functus amabilem
Ploravit omnis Antilochum senex
  Annos, nec impubem parentes 15
    Troilon aut Phrygiae sorores

Flevere semper. Desine mollium
Tandem querellarum, et potius nova

Cantemus Augusti tropaea
  Caesaris et rigidum Niphaten, 20

Medumque flumen gentibus additum
Victis minores volvere vertices,
  Intraque praescriptum Gelonos
    Exiguis equitare campis.

X.

Rectius vives, Licini, neque altum
Semper urgendo neque, dum procellas
Cautus horrescis, nimium premendo
  Litus iniquum.

Auream quisquis mediocritatem 5
Diligit, tutus caret obsoleti
Sordibus tecti, caret invidenda
  Sobrius aula.

Saepius ventis agitatur ingens
Pinus et celsae graviore casu 10
Decidunt turres feriuntque summos
  Fulgura montis.

Sperat infestis, metuit secundis
Alteram sortem bene praeparatum
Pectus. Informis hiemes reducit 15
  Iuppiter, idem

Submovet. Non, si male nunc, et olim
Sic erit: quondam cithara tacentem
Suscitat Musam neque semper arcum
  Tendit Apollo. 20

Rebus angustis animosus atque
Fortis appare; sapienter idem
Contrahes vento nimium secundo
  Turgida vela.

XI.

Quid bellicosus Cantaber et Scythes,
Hirpine Quinti, cogitet Hadria

Divisus obiecto, remittas
  Quaerere, nec trepides in usum

Poscentis aevi pauca. Fugit retro 5
Levis iuventas et decor, arida
  Pellente lascivos amores
    Canitie facilemque somnum.

Non semper idem floribus est honor
Vernis, neque uno luna rubens nitet 10
  Voltu: quid aeternis minorem
    Consiliis animum fatigas?

Cur non sub alta vel platano vel hac
Pinu iacentes sic temere et rosa
  Canos odorati capillos, 15
    Dum licet, Assyriaque nardo

Potamus uncti? Dissipat Euhius
Curas edacis. Quis puer ocius
  Restinguet ardentis Falerni
    Pocula praetereunte lympha? 20

Quis devium scortum eliciet domo
Lyden? Eburna, die age, cum lyra
  Maturet, in comptum Lacaenae
    More comam religata nodum.

XII.

Nolis longa ferae bella Numantiae
Nec durum Hannibalem nec Siculum mare
Poeno purpureum sanguine mollibus
  Aptari citharae modis,

Nec saevos Lapithas et nimium mero 5
Hylaeum domitosque Herculea manu
Telluris iuvenes, unde periculum
  Fulgens contremuit domus

Saturni veteris: tuque pedestribus
Dices historiis proelia Caesaris, 10
Maecenas, melius ductaque per vias
  Regum colla minacium.

Me dulcis dominae Musa Licymniae
Cantus, me voluit dicere lucidum

Fulgentis oculos et bene mutuis 15
  Fidum pectus amoribus;

Quam nec ferre pedem dedecuit choris
Nec certare ioco nec dare bracchia
Ludentem nitidis virginibus sacro
  Dianae celebris die. 20

Num tu quae tenuit dives Achaemenes
Aut pinguis Phrygiae Mygdonias opes
Permutare velis crine Licymniae,
  Plenas aut Arabum domos,

Dum flagrantia detorquet ad oscula 25
Cervicem, aut facili saevitia negat
Quae poscente magis gaudeat eripi,
  Interdum rapere occupet?

XIII.

Ille et nefasto te posuit die,
Quicumque primum, et sacrilega manu
  Produxit, arbos, in nepotum
    Perniciem opprobriumque pagi;

Illum et parentis crediderim sui 5
Fregisse cervicem et penetralia
  Sparsisse nocturno cruore
    Hospitis; ille venena Colcha

Et quidquid usquam concipitur nefas
Tractavit, agro qui statuit meo 10
  Te triste lignum, te caducum
    In domini caput immerentis.

Quid quisque vitet, numquam homini satis
Cautumst in horas: navita Bosporum
  Poenus perhorrescit neque ultra 15
    Caeca timet aliunde fata;

Miles sagittas et celerem fugam
Parthi, catenas Parthus et Italum
  Robur; sed improvisa leti
    Vis rapuit rapietque gentis. 20

Quam paene furvae regna Proserpinae
Et iudicantem vidimus Aeacum

Sedesque discriptas piorum et
　　Aeoliis fidibus querentem

Sappho puellis de popularibus, 25
Et te sonantem plenius aureo,
　　Alcaee, plectro dura navis,
　　　Dura fugae mala, dura belli.

Utrumque sacro digna silentio
Mirantur umbrae dicere; sed magis 30
　　Pugnas et exactos tyrannos
　　　Densum umeris bibit aure volgus.

Quid mirum, ubi illis carminibus stupens
Demittit atras belua centiceps
　　Auris, et intorti capillis 35
　　　Eumenidum recreantur angues?

Quin et Prometheus et Pelopis parens
Dulci laborem decipitur sono,
　　Nec curat Orion leones
　　　Aut timidos agitare lyncas. 40

XIV.

Eheu fugaces, Postume, Postume,
Labuntur anni, nec pietas moram
　　Rugis et instanti senectae
　　　Adferet indomitaeque morti;

Non si trecenis quotquot eunt dies, 5
Amice, places inlacrimabilem
　　Plutona tauris, qui ter amplum
　　　Geryonen Tityonque tristi

Compescit unda, scilicet omnibus,
Quicumque terrae munere vescimur, 10
　　Enaviganda, sive reges
　　　Sive inopes erimus coloni.

Frustra cruento Marte carebimus
Fractisque rauci fluctibus Hadriae,
　　Frustra per autumnos nocentem 15
　　　Corporibus metuemus Austrum:

Visendus ater flumine languido
Cocytos errans et Danai genus

Infame damnatusque longi
  Sisyphus Aeolides laboris. 20

Linquenda tellus et domus et placens
Uxor, neque harum, quas colis, arborum
  Te praeter invisas cupressos
    Ulla brevem dominum sequetur.

Absumet heres Caecuba dignior 25
Servata centum clavibus et mero
  Tinguet pavimentum superbo,
    Pontificum potiore cenis.

XV.

Iam pauca aratro iugera regiae
Moles relinquent; undique latius
  Extenta visentur Lucrino
    Stagna lacu, platanusque caelebs

Evincet ulmos; tum violaria et 5
Myrtus et omnis copia narium
  Spargent olivetis odorem
    Fertilibus domino priori;

Tum spissa ramis laurea fervidos
Excludet ictus. Non ita Romuli 10
  Praescriptum et intonsi Catonis
    Auspiciis veterumque norma.

Privatus illis census erat brevis,
Commune magnum: nulla decempedis
  Metata privatis opacam 15
    Porticus excipiebat Arcton,

Nec fortuitum spernere caespitem
Leges sinebant, oppida publico
  Sumptu iubentes et deorum
    Templa novo decorare saxo. 20

XVI.

Otium divos rogat in patenti
Prensus Aegaeo, simul atra nubes

Condidit lunam neque certa fulgent
  Sidera nautis;

Otium bello furiosa Thrace, 5
Otium Medi pharetra decori,
Grosphe, non gemmis neque purpura ve-
  nale nec auro.

Non enim gazae neque consularis
Submovet lictor miseros tumultus 10
Mentis et curas laqueata circum
  Tecta volantis.

Vivitur parvo bene cui paternum
Splendet in mensa tenui salinum
Nec levis somnos timor aut cupido 15
  Sordidus aufert.

Quid brevi fortes iaculamur aevo
Multa? Quid terras alio calentis
Sole mutamus? Patriae quis exsul
  Se quoque fugit? 20

Scandit aeratas vitiosa navis
Cura nec turmas equitum relinquit,
Ocior cervis et agente nimbos
  Ocior Euro.

Laetus in praesens animus quod ultrast 25
Oderit curare et amara lento
Temperet risu; nihil est ab omni
  Parte beatum.

Abstulit clarum cita mors Achillem,
Longa Tithonum minuit senectus, 30
Et mihi forsan tibi quod negarit
  Porriget hora.

Te greges centum Siculaeque circum
Mugiunt vaccae, tibi tollit hinnitum
Apta quadrigis equa, te bis Afro 35
  Murice tinctae

Vestiunt lanae; mihi parva rura et
Spiritum Graiae tenuem Camenae
Parca non mendax dedit et malignum
  Spernere volgus. 40

XVII.

Cur me querellis exanimas tuis?
Nec dis amicumst nec mihi te prius
  Obire, Maecenas, mearum
    Grande decus columenque rerum.

A, te meae si partem animae rapit 5
Maturior vis, quid moror altera,
  Nec carus aeque nec superstes
    Integer? Ille dies utramque

Ducet ruinam. Non ego perfidum
Dixi sacramentum: ibimus, ibimus, 10
  Utcumque praecedes, supremum
    Carpere iter comites parati.

Me nec Chimaerae spiritus igneae
Nec, si resurgat, centimanus Gyas
  Divellet umquam: sic potenti 15
    Iustitiae placitumque Parcis.

Seu Libra seu me Scorpios adspicit
Formidolosus pars violentior
  Natalis horae, seu tyrannus
    Hesperiae Capricornus undae, 20

Utrumque nostrum incredibili modo
Consentit astrum. Te Iovis impio
  Tutela Saturno refulgens
    Eripuit volucrisque Fati

Tardavit alas, cum populus frequens 25
Laetum theatris ter crepuit sonum;
  Me truncus inlapsus cerebro
    Sustulerat, nisi Faunus ictum

Dextra levasset, Mercurialium
Custos virorum. Reddere victimas 30
  Aedemque votivam memento;
    Nos humilem feriemus agnam.

XVIII.

Non ebur neque aureum
  Mea renidet in domo lacunar,

Non trabes Hymettiae
  Premunt columnas ultima recisas
Africa, neque Attali 5
  Ignotus heres regiam occupavi,
Nec Laconicas mihi
  Trahunt honestae purpuras clientae.
At fides et ingeni
  Benigna venast, pauperemque dives 10
Me petit: nihil supra
  Deos lacesso nec potentem amicum
Largiora flagito,
  Satis beatus unicis Sabinis.
Truditur dies die, 15
  Novaeque pergunt interire lunae:
Tu secanda marmora
  Locas sub ipsum funus, et sepulcri
Immemor struis domos,
  Marisque Bais obstrepentis urges 20
Submovere litora,
  Parum locuples continente ripa.
Quid quod usque proximos
  Revellis agri terminos et ultra
Limites clientium 25
  Salis avarus? Pellitur paternos
In sinu ferens deos
  Et uxor et vir sordidosque natos.
Nulla certior tamen
  Rapacis Orci fine destinata 30
Aula divitem manet
  Erum. Quid ultra tendis? Aequa tellus
Pauperi recluditur
  Regumque pueris, nec satelles Orci
Callidum Promethea 35
  Revexit auro captus. Hic superbum
Tantalum atque Tantali
  Genus coercet, hic levare functum
Pauperem laboribus
  Vocatus atque non vocatus audit. 40

XIX.

Bacchum in remotis carmina rupibus
Vidi docentem, credite posteri,
  Nymphasque discentis et auris
    Capripedum Satyrorum acutas.

Euhoe, recenti mens trepidat metu, 5
Plenoque Bacchi pectore turbidum
  Laetatur. Euhoe, parce Liber,
    Parce gravi metuende thyrso.

Fas pervicacis est mihi Thyiadas
Vinique fontem lactis et uberes 10
  Cantare rivos atque truncis
    Lapsa cavis iterare mella;

Fas et beatae coniugis additum
Stellis honorem tectaque Penthei
  Disiecta non leni ruina 15
    Thracis et exitium Lycurgi.

Tu flectis amnis, tu mare barbarum,
Tu separatis uvidus in iugis
  Nodo coerces viperino
    Bistonidum sine fraude crinis. 20

Tu, cum parentis regna per arduum
Cohors Gigantum scanderet impia,
  Rhoetum retorsisti leonis
    Unguibus horribilique mala;

Quamquam choreis aptior et iocis 25
Ludoque dictus non sat idoneus
  Pugnae ferebaris; sed idem
    Pacis eras mediusque belli.

Te vidit insons Cerberus aureo
Cornu decorum, leniter atterens 30
  Caudam, et recedentis trilingui
    Ore pedes tetigitque crura.

XX.

Non usitata nec tenui ferar
Penna biformis per liquidum aethera
  Vates, neque in terris morabor
    Longius invidiaque maior

Urbis relinquam. Non ego pauperum 5
Sanguis parentum, non ego, quem vocas,
  Dilecte Maecenas, obibo
    Nec Stygia cohibebor unda.

Iam iam residunt cruribus asperae
Pelles et album mutor in alitem 10
  Superne, nascunturque leves
    Per digitos umerosque plumae.

Iam Daedaleo notior Icaro
Visam gementis litora Bospori
  Syrtisque Gaetulas canorus 15
    Ales Hyperboreosque campos.

Me Colchus et qui dissimulat metum
Marsae cohortis Dacus et ultimi
  Noscent Geloni, me peritus
    Discet Hiber Rhodanique potor. 20

Absint inani funere neniae
Luctusque turpes et querimoniae;
  Compesce clamorem ac sepulcri
    Mitte supervacuos honores.

CARMINUM

LIBER TERTIUS.

I.

Odi profanum volgus et arceo.
Favete linguis: carmina non prius
  Audita Musarum sacerdos
    Virginibus puerisque canto.

Regum timendorum in proprios greges, 5
Reges in ipsos imperiumst Iovis,
  Clari Giganteo triumpho,
    Cuncta supercilio moventis.

Est ut viro vir latius ordinet
Arbusta sulcis, hic generosior 10
  Descendat in Campum petitor,
    Moribus hic meliorque fama

Contendat, illi turba clientium
Sit maior: aequa lege Necessitas

Sortitur insignis et imos; 15
   Omne capax movet urna nomen.

Destrictus ensis cui super impia
Cervice pendet, non Siculae dapes
   Dulcem elaborabunt saporem,
      Non avium citharaeque cantus 20

Somnum reducent. Somnus agrestium
Lenis virorum non humilis domos
   Fastidit umbrosamque ripam,
      Non zephyris agitata tempe.

Desiderantem quod satis est neque 25
Tumultuosum sollicitat mare
   Nec saevus Arcturi cadentis
      Impetus aut orientis Haedi,

Non verberatae grandine vineae
Fundusque mendax, arbore nunc aquas 30
   Culpante, nunc torrentia agros
      Sidera, nunc hiemes iniquas.

Contracta pisces aequora sentiunt
Iactis in altum molibus: huc frequens
   Caementa demittit redemptor 35
      Cum famulis dominusque terrae

Fastidiosus. Sed Timor et Minae
Scandunt eodem quo dominus, neque
   Decedit aerata triremi et
      Post equitem sedet atra Cura. 40

Quod si dolentem nec Phrygius lapis
Nec purpurarum sidere clarior
   Delenit usus nec Falerna
      Vitis Achaemeniumque costum:

Cur invidendis postibus et novo 45
Sublime ritu moliar atrium?
   Cur valle permutem Sabina
      Divitias operosiores?

II.

Angustam amice pauperiem pati
Robustus acri militia puer

Condiscat et Parthos ferocis
  Vexet eques metuendus hasta,

Vitamque sub divo et trepidis agat 5
In rebus. Illum ex moenibus hosticis
  Matrona bellantis tyranni
    Prospiciens et adulta virgo

Suspiret, eheu, ne rudis agminum
Sponsus lacessat regius asperum 10
  Tactu leonem, quem cruenta
    Per medias rapit ira caedes.

Dulce et decorumst pro patria mori:
Mors et fugacem persequitur virum,
  Nec parcit imbellis iuventae 15
    Poplitibus timidoque tergo.

Virtus repulsae nescia sordidae,
Intaminatis fulget honoribus,
  Nec sumit aut ponit securis
    Arbitrio popularis aurae. 20

Virtus recludens immeritis mori
Caelum negata temptat iter via,
  Coetusque volgaris et udam
    Spernit humum fugiente penna.

Est et fideli tuta silentio 25
Merces: vetabo qui Cereris sacrum
  Volgarit arcanae sub isdem
    Sit trabibus fragilemve mecum

Solvat phaselon; saepe Diespiter
Neglectus incesto addidit integrum: 30
  Raro antecedentem scelestum
    Deseruit pede Poena claudo.

III.

Iustum et tenacem propositi virum
Non civium ardor prava iubentium,
  Non voltus instantis tyranni
    Mente quatit solida, neque Auster,

Dux inquieti turbidus Hadriae, 5
Nec fulminantis magna manus Iovis;

Si fractus inlabatur orbis,
   Impavidum ferient ruinae.

Hac arte Pollux et vagus Hercules
Enisus arcis attigit igneas, 10
   Quos inter Augustus recumbens
    Purpureo bibet ore nectar.

Hac te merentem, Bacche pater, tuae
Vexere tigres, indocili iugum
   Collo trahentes; hac Quirinus 15
    Martis equis Acheronta fugit,

Gratum elocuta consiliantibus
Iunone divis: 'Ilion, Ilion
   Fatalis incestusque iudex
    Et mulier peregrina vertit 20

In pulverem, ex quo destituit deos
Mercede pacta Laomedon, mihi
   Castaeque damnatum Minervae
    Cum populo et duce fraudulento.

Iam nec Lacaenae splendet adulterae 25
Famosus hospes nec Priami domus
   Periura pugnacis Achivos
    Hectoreis opibus refringit,

Nostrisque ductum seditionibus
Bellum resedit. Protinus et gravis 30
   Iras et invisum nepotem,
    Troica quem peperit sacerdos,

Marti redonabo; illum ego lucidas
Inire sedes, ducere nectaris
   Sucos et adscribi quietis 35
    Ordinibus patiar deorum.

Dum longus inter saeviat Ilion
Romamque pontus, qualibet exsules
   In parte regnanto beati;
    Dum Priami Paridisque busto 40

Insultet armentum et catulos ferae
Celent inultae, stet Capitolium
   Fulgens triumphatisque possit
    Roma ferox dare iura Medis.

Horrenda late nomen in ultimas 45
Extendat oras, qua medius liquor

Secernit Europen ab Afro,
  Qua tumidus rigat arva Nilus.

Aurum inrepertum et sic melius situm,
Cum terra celat, spernere fortior 50
  Quam cogere humanos in usus
    Omne sacrum rapiente dextra,

Quicumque mundo terminus obstitit,
Hunc tanget armis, visere gestiens,
  Qua parte debacchentur ignes, 55
    Qua nebulae pluviique rores.

Sed bellicosis fata Quiritibus
Hac lege dico, ne nimium pii
  Rebusque fidentes avitae
    Tecta velint reparare Troiae. 60

Troiae renascens alite lugubri
Fortuna tristi clade iterabitur,
  Ducente victricis catervas
    Coniuge me Iovis et sorore.

Ter si resurgat murus aeneus 65
Auctore Phoebo, ter pereat meis
  Excisus Argivis, ter uxor
    Capta virum puerosque ploret.'

Non hoc iocosae conveniet lyrae:
Quo, Musa, tendis? Desine pervicax 70
  Referre sermones deorum et
    Magna modis tenuare parvis.

IV.

Descende caelo et dic age tibia
Regina longum Calliope melos,
  Seu voce nunc mavis acuta,
    Seu fidibus citharave Phoebi.

Auditis, an me ludit amabilis 5
Insania? Audire et videor pios
  Errare per lucos, amoenae
    Quos et aquae subeunt et aurae.

Me fabulosae Volture in Apulo
Nutricis extra limen Apuliae 10

Ludo fatigatumque somno
   Fronde nova puerum palumbes

Texere, mirum quod foret omnibus,
Quicumque celsae nidum Acherontiae
   Saltusque Bantinos et arvum 15
     Pingue tenent humilis Forenti,

Ut tuto ab atris corpore viperis
Dormirem et ursis, ut premerer sacra
   Lauroque conlataque myrto,
     Non sine dis animosus infans. 20

Vester, Camenae, vester in arduos
Tollor Sabinos, seu mihi frigidum
   Praeneste seu Tibur supinum
     Seu liquidae placuere Baiae.

Vestris amicum fontibus et choris 25
Non me Philippis versa acies retro,
   Devota non extinxit arbos,
     Nec Sicula Palinurus unda.

Utcumque mecum vos eritis, libens
Insanientem navita Bosporum 30
   Temptabo et urentis arenas
     Litoris Assyrii viator;

Visam Britannos hospitibus feros
Et laetum equino sanguine Concanum;
   Visam pharetratos Gelonos 35
     Et Scythicum inviolatus amnem.

Vos Caesarem altum, militia simul
Fessas cohortis abdidit oppidis,
   Finire quaerentem labores,
     Pierio recreatis antro. 40

Vos lene consilium et datis et dato
Gaudetis, almae. Scimus, ut impios
   Titanas immanemque turmam
     Fulmine sustulerit caduco

Qui terram inertem, qui mare temperat 45
Ventosum et urbis regnaque tristia
   Divosque mortalisque turbas
     Imperio regit unus aequo.

Magnum illa terrorem intulerat Iovi
Fidens iuventus horrida bracchiis, 50

Fratresque tendentes opaco
  Pelion imposuisse Olympo.

Sed quid Typhoeus et validus Mimas,
Aut quid minaci Porphyrion statu,
  Quid Rhoetus evolsisque truncis 55
    Enceladus iaculator audax

Contra sonantem Palladis aegida
Possent ruentes? Hinc avidus stetit
  Volcanus, hinc matrona Iuno et
    Numquam umeris positurus arcum, 60

Qui rore puro Castaliae lavit
Crinis solutos, qui Lyciae tenet
  Dumeta natalemque silvam,
    Delius et Patareus Apollo.

Vis consili expers mole ruit sua: 65
Vim temperatam di quoque provehunt
  In maius; idem odere viris
    Omne nefas animo moventis.

Testis mearum centimanus Gyas
Sententiarum, notus et integrae 70
  Temptator Orion Dianae,
    Virginea domitus sagitta.

Iniecta monstris Terra dolet suis
Maeretque partus fulmine luridum
  Missos ad Orcum; nec peredit 75
    Impositam celer ignis Aetnam.

Incontinentis nec Tityi iecur
Reliquit ales, nequitiae additus
  Custos; amatorem trecentae
    Pirithoum cohibent catenae. 80

V.

Caelo tonantem credidimus Iovem
Regnare; praesens divus habebitur
  Augustus adiectis Britannis
    Imperio gravibusque Persis.

Milesne Crassi coniuge barbara 5
Turpis maritus vixit et hostium,

Pro curia inversique mores!
  Consenuit socerorum in armis

Sub rege Medo Marsus et Apulus,
Anciliorum et nominis et togae 10
  Oblitus aeternaeque Vestae,
    Incolumi Iove et urbe Roma?

Hoc caverat mens provida Reguli
Dissentientis condicionibus
  Foedis et exemplo trahentis 15
    Perniciem veniens in aevum,

Si non periret immiserabilis
Captiva pubes. 'Signa ego Punicis
  Adfixa delubris et arma
    Militibus sine caede' dixit 20

'Derepta vidi; vidi ego civium
Retorta tergo bracchia libero
  Portasque non clausas et arva
    Marte coli populata nostro.

Auro repensus scilicet acrior 25
Miles redibit. Flagitio additis
  Damnum: neque amissos colores
    Lana refert medicata fuco,

Nec vera virtus, cum semel excidit,
Curat reponi deterioribus. 30
  Si pugnat extricata densis
    Cerva plagis, erit ille fortis,

Qui perfidis se credidit hostibus,
Et Marte Poenos proteret altero
  Qui lora restrictis lacertis 35
    Sensit iners timuitque mortem.

Hic, unde vitam sumeret inscius,
Pacem duello miscuit. O pudor!
  O magna Carthago, probrosis
    Altior Italiae ruinis!' 40

Fertur pudicae coniugis osculum
Parvosque natos ut capitis minor
  Ab se removisse et virilem
    Torvus humi posuisse voltum,

Donec labantis consilio patres 45
Firmaret auctor numquam alias dato,

Interque maerentis amicos
  Egregius properaret exsul.

Atqui sciebat quae sibi barbarus
Tortor pararet; non aliter tamen 50
  Dimovit obstantis propinquos
    Et populum reditus morantem,

Quam si clientum longa negotia
Diiudicata lite relinqueret,
  Tendens Venafranos in agros 55
    Aut Lacedaemonium Tarentum.

VI.

Delicta maiorum immeritus lues,
Romane, donec templa refeceris
  Aedisque labentis deorum et
    Foeda nigro simulacra fumo.

Dis te minorem quod geris, imperas: 5
Hinc omne principium, huc refer exitum.
  Di multa neglecti dederunt
    Hesperiae mala luctuosae.

Iam bis Monaeses et Pacori manus
Non auspicatos contudit impetus 10
  Nostros et adiecisse praedam
    Torquibus exiguis renidet.

Paene occupatam seditionibus
Delevit Urbem Dacus et Aethiops,
  Hic classe formidatus, ille 15
    Missilibus melior sagittis.

Fecunda culpae saecula nuptias
Primum inquinavere et genus et domos
  Hoc fonte derivata clades
    In patriam populumque fluxit. 20

Motus doceri gaudet Ionicos
Matura virgo et fingitur artibus
  Iam nunc et incestos amores
    De tenero meditatur ungui.

Mox iuniores quaerit adulteros 25
Inter mariti vina, neque eligit

Cui donet impermissa raptim
  Gaudia luminibus remotis,

Sed iussa coram non sine conscio
Surgit marito, seu vocat institor 30
  Seu navis Hispanae magister,
    Dedecorum pretiosus emptor.

Non his iuventus orta parentibus
Infecit aequor sanguine Punico
  Pyrrhumque et ingentem cecidit 35
    Antiochum Hannibalemque dirum;

Sed rusticorum mascula militum
Proles, Sabellis docta ligonibus
  Versare glaebas et severae
    Matris ad arbitrium recisos 40

Portare fustis, sol ubi montium
Mutaret umbras et iuga demeret
  Bobus fatigatis amicum
    Tempus agens abeunte curru.

Damnosa quid non imminuit dies? 45
Aetas parentum, peior avis, tulit
  Nos nequiores, mox daturos
    Progeniem vitiosiorem.

VII.

Quid fles, Asterie, quem tibi candidi
Primo restituent vere Favonii
  Thyna merce beatum,
    Constantis iuvenem fide,

Gygen? Ille Notis actus ad Oricum 5
Post insana Caprae sidera frigidas
  Noctis non sine multis
    Insomnis lacrimis agit.

Atqui sollicitae nuntius hospitae,
Suspirare Chloen et miseram tuis 10
  Dicens ignibus uri,
    Temptat mille vafer modis.

Ut Proetum mulier perfida credulum
Falsis impulerit criminibus nimis

Casto Bellerophontae 15
  Maturare necem refert;

Narrat paene datum Pelea Tartaro,
Magnessam Hippolyten dum fugit abstinens;
  Et peccare docentis
    Fallax historias movet. 20

Frustra: nam scopulis surdior Icari
Voces audit adhuc integer. At tibi
  Ne vicinus Enipeus
    Plus iusto placeat cave;

Quamvis non alius flectere equum sciens 25
Aeque conspicitur gramine Martio,
  Nec quisquam citus aeque
    Tusco denatat alveo.

Prima nocte domum claude neque in vias
Sub cantu querulae despice tibiae, 30
  Et te saepe vocanti
    Duram difficilis mane.

VIII.

Martiis caelebs quid agam Kalendis,
Quid velint flores et acerra turis
Plena miraris positusque carbo in
  Caespite vivo,

Docte sermones utriusque linguae? 5
Voveram dulcis epulas et album
Libero caprum prope funeratus
  Arboris ictu.

Hic dies, anno redeunte festus,
Corticem adstrictum pice demovebit 10
Amphorae fumum bibere institutae
  Consule Tullo.

Sume, Maecenas, cyathos amici
Sospitis centum et vigiles lucernas
Perfer in lucem; procul omnis esto 15
  Clamor et ira.

Mitte civilis super urbe curas:
Occidit Daci Cotisonis agmen,

Medus infestus sibi luctuosis
  Dissidet armis, 20

Servit Hispanae vetus hostis orae
Cantaber sera domitus catena,
Iam Scythae laxo meditantur arcu
  Cedere campis.

Neglegens ne qua populus laboret, 25
Parce privatus nimium cavere;
Dona praesentis cape laetus horae,
  Linque severa.

IX.

'Donec gratus eram tibi
  Nec quisquam potior bracchia candidae
Cervici iuvenis dabat,
  Persarum vigui rege beatior.'

'Donec non alia magis 5
  Arsisti neque erat Lydia post Chloen,
Multi Lydia nominis
  Romana vigui clarior Ilia.'

'Me nunc Thressa Chloe regit,
  Dulcis docta modos et citharae sciens, 10
Pro qua non metuam mori,
  Si parcent animae fata superstiti.'

'Me torret face mutua
  Thurini Calais filius Ornyti,
Pro quo bis patiar mori, 15
  Si parcent puero fata superstiti.'

'Quid si prisca redit Venus
  Diductosque iugo cogit aeneo?
Si flava excutitur Chloe
  Reiectaeque patet ianua Lydiae?' 20

'Quamquam sidere pulchrior
  Illest, tu levior cortice et improbo
Iracundior Hadria,
  Tecum vivere amem, tecum obeam libens!'

X.

Extremum Tanain si biberes, Lyce,
Saevo nupta viro, me tamen asperas
  Porrectum ante foris obicere incolis
    Plorares Aquilonibus.

Audis, quo strepitu ianua, quo nemus 5
Inter pulchra satum tecta remugiat
  Ventis, et positas ut glaciet nivis
    Puro numine Iuppiter?

Ingratam Veneri porie superbiam,
Ne currente retro funis eat rota: 10
  Non te Penelopen difficilem procis
    Tyrrhenus genuit parens.

O quamvis neque te munera nec preces
Nec tinctus viola pallor amantium
  Nec vir Pieria paelice saucius 15
    Curvat, supplicibus tuis

Parcas, nec rigida mollior aesculo
Nec Mauris animum mitior anguibus.
  Non hoc semper erit liminis aut aquae
    Caelestis patiens latus. 20

XI.

Mercuri, nam te docilis magistro
Movit Amphion lapides canendo,
Tuque testudo resonare septem
  Callida nervis,

Nec loquax olim neque grata, nunc et 5
Divitum mensis et amica templis,
Dic modos Lyde quibus obstinatas
  Adplicet auris,

Quae velut latis equa trima campis
Ludit exsultim metuitque tangi, 10
Nuptiarum expers et adhuc protervo
  Cruda marito.

Tu potes tigris comitesque silvas
Ducere et rivos celeres morari;

Cessit immanis tibi blandienti 15
  Ianitor aulae

Cerberus, quamvis furiale centum
Muniant angues caput, eius atque
Spiritus taeter saniesque manet
  Ore trilingui. 20

Quin et Ixion Tityosque voltu
Risit invito; stetit urna paullum
Sicca, dum grato Danai puellas
  Carmine mulces.

Audiat Lyde scelus atque notas 25
Virginum poenas et inane lymphae
Dolium fundo pereuntis imo,
  Seraque fata

Quae manent culpas etiam sub Orco.
Impiae, (nam quid potuere maius?) 30
Impiae sponsos potuere duro
  Perdere ferro.

Una de multis face nuptiali
Digna periurum fuit in parentem
Splendide mendax et in omne virgo 35
  Nobilis aevum;

'Surge' quae dixit iuveni marito,
'Surge, ne longus tibi somnus, unde
Non times, detur; socerum et scelestas
  Falle sorores, 40

Quae, velut nactae vitulos leaenae,
Singulos eheu lacerant. Ego illis
Mollior nec te feriam neque intra
  Claustra tenebo.

Me pater saevis oneret catenis, 45
Quod viro clemeus misero peperci;
Me vel extremos Numidarum in agros
  Classe releget.

I pedes quo te rapiunt et aurae,
Dum favet nox et Venus, i secundo 50
Omine et nostri memorem sepulcro
  Scalpe querellam.'

XII.

Miserarumst neque amori dare ludum neque dulci
Mala vino lavere, aut exanimari metuentis
Patruae verbera linguae.

Tibi qualum Cythereae puer ales, tibi telas
Operosaeque Minervae studium aufert, Neobule, 5
Liparaei nitor Hebri

Simul unctos Tiberinis umeros lavit in undis,
Eques ipso melior Bellerophonte, neque pugno
Neque segni pede victus;

Catus idem per apertum fugientis agitato 10
Grege cervos iaculari et celer arto latitantem
Fruticeto excipere aprum.

XIII.

O fons Bandusiae, splendidior vitro,
Dulci digne mero non sine floribus,
  Cras donaberis haedo,
    Cui frons turgida cornibus

Primis et venerem et proelia destinat; 5
Frustra: nam gelidos inficiet tibi
  Rubro sanguine rivos,
    Lascivi suboles gregis.

Te flagrantis atrox hora Caniculae
Nescit tangere, tu frigus amabile 10
  Fessis vomere tauris
    Praebes et pecori vago.

Fies nobilium tu quoque fontium,
Me dicente cavis impositam ilicem
  Saxis unde loquaces 15
    Lymphae desiliunt tuae.

XIV.

Herculis ritu modo dictus, o plebs,
Morte venalem petiisse laurum,
Caesar Hispana repetit penatis
  Victor ab ora.

Unico gaudens mulier marito 5
Prodeat iustis operata divis
Et soror clari ducis et decorae
  Supplice vitta

Virginum matres iuvenumque nuper
Sospitum. Vos, o pueri et puellae 10
Iam virum expertae, male ominatis
  Parcite verbis.

Hic dies vere mihi festus atras
Eximet curas; ego nec tumultum
Nec mori per vim metuam tenente 15
  Caesare terras.

I, pete unguentum, puer, et coronas
Et cadum Marsi memorem duelli,
Spartacum si qua potuit vagantem
  Fallere testa. 20

Dic et argutae properet Neaerae
Murreum nodo cohibere crinem;
Si per invisum mora ianitorem
  Fiet, abito.

Lenit albescens animos capillus 25
Litium et rixae cupidos protervae;
Non ego hoc ferrem calidus iuventa
  Consule Planco.

XV.

Uxor pauperis Ibyci,
  Tandem nequitiae fige modum tuae
Famosisque laboribus:
  Maturo propior desine funeri
Inter ludere virgines, 5
  Et stellis nebulam spargere candidis.
Non, siquid Pholoen satis,
  Et te, Chlori, decet: filia rectius
Expugnat iuvenum domos,
  Pulso Thyias uti concita tympano. 10

Illam cogit amor Nothi
  Lascivae similem ludere capreae;
Te lanae prope nobilem
  Tonsae Luceriam, non citharae decent
Nec flos purpureus rosae 15
  Nec poti vetulam faece tenus cadi.

XVI.

Inclusam Danaen turris aenea
Robustaeque fores et vigilum canum
  Tristes excubiae munierant satis
    Nocturnis ab adulteris,

Si non Acrisium virginis abditae 5
Custodem pavidum Iuppiter et Venus
  Risissent: fore enim tutum iter et patens
    Converso in pretium deo.

Aurum per medios ire satellites
Et perrumpere amat saxa potentius 10
  Ictu fulmineo: concidit auguris
    Argivi domus, ob lucrum

Demersa exitio; diffidit urbium
Portas vir Macedo et subruit aemulos
  Reges muneribus; munera navium 15
    Saevos inlaqueant duces.

Crescentem sequitur cura pecuniam
Maiorumque fames. Iure perhorrui
  Late conspicuum tollere verticem,
    Maecenas, equitum decus. 20

Quanto quisque sibi plura negaverit,
Ab dis plura feret. Nil cupientium
  Nudus castra peto et transfuga divitum
    Partis linquere gestio,

Contemptae dominus splendidior rei, 25
Quam si quidquid arat impiger Apulus
  Occultare meis dicerer horreis,
    Magnas inter opes inops.

Purae rivus aquae silvaque iugerum
Paucorum et segetis certa fides meae 30

Fulgentem imperio fertilis Africae
   Fallit sorte beatior.

Quamquam nec Calabrae mella ferunt apes,
Nec Laestrygonia Bacchus in amphora
   Languescit mihi, nec pinguia Gallicis 35
    Crescunt vellera pascuis;

Importuna tamen pauperies abest,
Nec si plura velim tu dare deneges.
   Contracto melius parva cupidine
    Vectigalia porrigam, 40

Quam si Mygdoniis regnum Alyattei
Campis continuem. Multa petentibus
   Desunt multa: benest, cui deus obtulit
    Parca quod satis est manu.

XVII.

Aeli vetusto nobilis ab Lamo,
Qnando et priores hinc Lamias ferunt
   Denominatos et nepotum
    Per memores genus omne fastos;

Auctore ab illo ducis originem 5
Qui Formiarum moenia dicitur
   Princeps et innantem Maricae
    Litoribus tenuisse Lirim,

Late tyrannus:—cras foliis nemus
Multis et alga litus inutili 10
   Demissa tempestas ab Euro
    Sternet, aquae nisi fallit augur

Annosa cornix. Dum potes, aridum
Compone lignum: cras Genium mero
   Curabis et porco bimenstri 15
    Cum famulis operum solutis.

XVIII.

Faune, Nympharum fugientum amator,
Per meos finis et aprica rura

Lenis incedas, abeasque parvis
　Aequus alumnis,

Si tener pleno cadit haedus anno, 5
Larga nec desunt Veneris sodali
Vina craterae, vetus ara multo
　Fumat odore.

Ludit herboso pecus omne campo,
Cum tibi Nonae redeunt Decembres; 10
Festus in pratis vacat otioso
　Cum bove pagus;

Inter audacis lupus errat agnos;
Spargit agrestis tibi silva frondis;
Gaudet invisam pepulisse fossor 15
　Ter pede terram.

XIX.

Quantum distet ab Inacho
　Codrus pro patria non timidus mori
Narras et genus Aeaci
　Et pugnata sacro bella sub Ilio;
Quo Chium pretio cadum 5
　Mercemur, quis aquam temperet ignibus,
Quo praebente domum et quota
　Paelignis caream frigoribus, taces.
Da lunae propere novae,
　Da noctis mediae, da, puer, auguris 10
Murenae: tribus aut novem
　Miscentur cyathis pocula commodis.
Qui Musas amat imparis,
　Ternos ter cyathos attonitus petet
Vates; tris prohibet supra 15
　Rixarum metuens tangere Gratia
Nudis iuncta sororibus.
　Insanire iuvat: cur Berecyntiae
Cessant flamina tibiae?
　Cur pendet tacita fistula cum lyra? 20
Parcentis ego dexteras
　Odi: sparge rosas; audiat invidus
Dementem strepitum Lycus
　Et vicina seni non habilis Lyco.
Spissa te nitidum coma, 25
　Puro te similem, Telephe, Vespero

Tempestiva petit Rhode;
  Me lentus Glycerae torret amor meae.

XX.

Non vides quanto moveas periclo,
Pyrrhe, Gaetulae catulos leaenae?
Dura post paullo fugies inaudax
  Proelia raptor,

Cum per obstantis iuvenum catervas 5
Ibit insignem repetens Nearchum:
Grande certamen, tibi praeda cedat
  Maior an illi.

Interim, dum tu celeres sagittas
Promis, haec dentis acuit timendos, 10
Arbiter pugnae posuisse nudo
  Sub pede palmam

Fertur et leni recreare vento
Sparsum odoratis umerum capillis,
Qualis aut Nireus fuit aut aquosa 15
  Raptus ab Ida.

XXI.

O nata mecum consule Manlio,
Seu tu querellas sive geris iocos
  Seu rixam et insanos amores
    Seu facilem, pia testa, somnum,

Quocumque lectum nomiue Massicum 5
Servas, moveri digna bono die,
  Descende, Corvino iubente
    Promere languidiora vina.

Non ille, quamquam Socraticis madet
Sermonibus, te negleget horridus: 10
  Narratur et prisci Catonis
    Saepe mero caluisse virtus.

Tu lene tormentum ingenio admoves
Plerumque duro; tu sapientium

Curas et arcanum iocoso 15
  Consilium retegis Lyaeo;

Tu spem reducis mentibus anxiis
Virisque et addis cornua pauperi,
  Post te neque iratos trementi
    Regum apices neque militum arma. 20

Te Liber et, si laeta aderit, Venus
Segnesque nodum solvere Gratiae
  Vivaeque producent lucernae,
    Dum rediens fugat astra Phoebus.

XXII.

Montium custos nemorumque Virgo,
Quae laborantis utero puellas
Ter vocata audis adimisque leto,
  Diva triformis,

Imminens villae tua pinus esto, 5
Quam per exactos ego laetus annos
Verris obliquum meditantis ictum
  Sanguine donem.

XXIII.

Caelo supinas si tuleris manus
Nascente luna, rustica Phidyle,
  Si ture placaris et horna
    Fruge Laris avidaque porca,

Nec pestilentem sentiet Africum 5
Fecunda vitis nec sterilem seges
  Robiginem aut dulces alumni
    Pomifero grave tempus anno.

Nam quae nivali pascitur Algido
Devota quercus inter et ilices 10
  Aut crescit Albanis in herbis
    Victima pontificum securis

Cervice tinguet: te nihil attinet
Temptare multa caede bidentium

Parvos coronantem marino 15
  Rore deos fragilique myrto.

Immunis aram si tetigit manus,
Non sumptuosa blandior hostia
  Mollivit aversos Penatis
    Farre pio et saliente mica. 20

XXIV.

Intactis opulentior
  Thesauris Arabum et divitis Indiae
Caementis licet occupes
  Tyrrhenum omne tuis et mare Apulicum,
Si figit adamantinos 5
  Summis verticibus dira Necessitas
Clavos, non animum metu,
  Non mortis laqueis expedies caput.
Campestres melius Scythae,
  Quorum plaustra vagas rite trahunt domos, 10
Vivunt et rigidi Getae,
  Immetata quibus iugera liberas
Fruges et Cererem ferunt,
  Nec cultura placet longior annua,
Defunctumque laboribus 15
  Aequali recreat sorte vicarius.
Illic matre carentibus
  Privignis mulier temperat innocens,
Nec dotata regit virum
  Coniunx nec nitido fidit adultero; 20
Dos est magna parentium
  Virtus et metuens alterius viri
Certo foedere castitas,
  Et peccare nefas aut pretiumst mori.
O quisquis volet impias 25
  Caedis et rabiem tollere civicam,
Si quaeret pater urbium
  Subscribi statuis, indomitam audeat
Refrenare licentiam,
  Clarus post genitis: quatenus, heu nefas! 30
Virtutem incolumem odimus,
  Sublatam ex oculis quaerimus invidi.
Quid tristes querimoniae,
  Si non supplicio culpa reciditur;
Quid leges sine moribus 35
  Vanae proficiunt, si neque fervidis
Pars inclusa caloribus
  Mundi nec boreae finitimum latus

Durataeque solo nives
  Mercatorem abigunt, horrida callidi 40
Vincunt aequora navitae,
  Magnum pauperies opprobrium iubet
Quidvis et facere et pati,
  Virtutisque viam deserit arduae?
Vel nos in Capitolium, 45
  Quo clamor vocat et turba faventium,
Vel nos in mare proximum
  Gemmas et lapides aurum et inutile,
Summi materiem mali,
  Mittamus, scelerum si bene paenitet. 50
Eradenda cupidinis
  Pravi sunt elementa et tenerae nimis
Mentes asperioribus
  Formandae studiis. Nescit equo rudis
Haerere ingenuus puer 55
  Venarique timet, ludere doctior,
Seu Graeco iubeas trocho,
  Seu malis vetita legibus alea,
Cum periura patris fides
  Consortem socium fallat et hospites, 60
Indignoque pecuniam
  Heredi properet. Scilicet improbae
Crescunt divitiae; tamen
  Curtae nescio quid semper abest rei.

XXV.

Quo me, Bacche, rapis tui
  Plenum? Quae nemora aut quos agor in specus,
Velox mente nova? Quibus
  Antris egregii Caesaris audiar
Aeternum meditans decus 5
  Stellis inserere et consilio Iovis?
Dicam insigne, recens, adhuc
  Indictum ore alio. Non secus in iugis
Exsomnis stupet Euhias,
  Hebrum prospiciens et nive candidam 10
Thracen ac pede barbaro
  Lustratam Rhodopen, ut mihi devio
Ripas et vacuum nemus
  Mirari libet. O Naiadum potens
Baccharumque valentium 15
  Proceras manibus vertere fraxinos,
Nil parvum aut humili modo,
  Nil mortale loquar. Dulce periculumst,

O Lenaee, sequi deum
  Cingentem viridi tempora pampino. 20

XXVI.

Vixi puellis nuper idoneus
Et militavi non sine gloria;
  Nunc arma defunctumque bello
    Barbiton hic paries habebit,

Laevum marinae qui Veneris latus 5
Custodit. Hic, hic ponite lucida
  Funalia et vectis et arcus
    Oppositis foribus minacis,

O quae beatam diva tenes Cyprum et
Memphin carentem Sithonia nive, 10
  Regina, sublimi flagello
    Tange Chloen semel arrogantem.

XXVII.

Impios parrae recinentis omen
Ducat et praegnans canis aut ab agro
Rava decurrens lupa Lanuvino
    Fetaque volpes;

Rumpat et serpens iter institutum, 5
Si per obliquum similis sagittae
Terruit mannos: ego cui timebo,
  Providus auspex,

Antequam stantis repetat paludes
Imbrium divina avis imminentum, 10
Oscinem corvum prece suscitabo
  Solis ab ortu.

Sis licet felix, ubicumque mavis,
Et memor nostri, Galatea, vivas;
Teque nec laevus vetet ire picus 15
  Nec vaga cornix.

Sed vides quanto trepidet tumultu
Pronus Orion. Ego quid sit ater

Hadriae novi sinus et quid albus
  Peccet Iapyx. 20

Hostium uxores puerique caecos
Sentiant motus orientis Austri et
Aequoris nigri fremitum et trementis
  Verbere ripas.

Sic et Europe niveum doloso 25
Credidit tauro latus et scatentem
Beluis pontum mediasque fraudes
  Palluit audax:

Nuper in pratis studiosa florum et
Debitae Nymphis opifex coronae 30
Nocte sublustri nihil astra praeter
  Vidit et undas.

Quae simul centum tetigit potentem
Oppidis Creten, 'Pater—o relictum
Filiae nomen pietasque' dixit, 35
  'Victa furore!

Unde quo veni? Levis una mors est
Virginum culpae. Vigilansne ploro
Turpe commissum an vitiis carentem
  Ludit imago 40

Vana quae porta fugiens eburna
Somnium ducit? Meliusne fluctus
Ire per longos fuit, an recentis
  Carpere flores?

Siquis infamem mihi nunc iuvencum 45
Dedat iratae, lacerare ferro et
Frangere enitar modo multum amati
  Cornua monstri.

Impudens liqui patrios Penatis,
Impudens Orcum moror. O deorum 50
Siquis haec audis, utinam inter errem
  Nuda leones!

Antequam turpis macies decentis
Occupet malas teneraeque sucus
Defluat praedae, speciosa quaero 55
  Pascere tigris.

Vilis Europe, pater urget absens:
Quid mori cessas? Potes hac ab orno

Pendulum zona bene te secuta
  Laedere collum. 60

Sive te rupes et acuta leto
Saxa delectant, age te procellae
Crede veloci, nisi erile mavis
  Carpere pensum

Regius sanguis, dominaeque tradi 65
Barbarae paelex.' Aderat querenti
Perfidum ridens Venus et remisso
  Filius arcu.

Mox ubi lusit satis, 'abstineto'
Dixit 'irarum calidaeque rixae, 70
Cum tibi invisus laceranda reddet
  Cornua taurus.

Uxor invicti Iovis esse nescis.
Mitte singultus, bene ferre magnam
Disce fortunam; tua sectus orbis 75
  Nomina ducet.'

XXVIII.

Festo quid potius die
  Neptuni faciam? Prome reconditum,
Lyde strenua Caecubum,
  Munitaeque adhibe vim sapientiae.
Inclinare meridiem 5
  Sentis et, veluti stet volucris dies,
Parcis deripere horreo
  Cessantem Bibuli consulis amphoram.
Nos cantabimus invicem
  Neptunum et viridis Nereidum comas; 10
Tu curva recines lyra
  Latonam et celeris spicula Cynthiae:
Summo carmine quae Cnidon
  Fulgentisque tenet Cycladas, et Paphum
Iunctis visit oloribus; 15
  Dicetur merita Nox quoque nenia.

XXIX.

Tyrrhena regum progenies, tibi
Non ante verso lene merum cado
  Cum flore, Maecenas, rosarum et
    Pressa tuis balanus capillis

Iamdudum apud mest: eripe te morae, 5
Ne semper udum Tibur et Aefulae
  Declive contempleris arvum et
    Telegoni iuga parricidae.

Fastidiosam desere copiam et
Molem propinquam nubibus arduis, 10
  Omitte mirari beatae
    Fumum et opes strepitumque Romae.

Plerumque gratae divitibus vices
Mundaeque parvo sub lare pauperum
  Cenae sine aulaeis et ostro 15
    Sollicitam explicuere frontem.

Iam clarus occultum Andromedae pater
Ostendit ignem, iam Procyon furit
  Et stella vesani Leonis,
    Sole dies referente siccos; 20

Iam pastor umbras cum grege languido
Rivumque fessus quaerit et horridi
  Dumeta Silvani, caretque
    Ripa vagis taciturna ventis.

Tu civitatem quis deceat status 25
Curas et Urbi sollicitus times
  Quid Seres et regnata Cyro
    Bactra parent Tanaisque discors.

Prudens futuri temporis egitum
Caliginosa nocte premit deus, 30
  Ridetque si mortalis ultra
    Fas trepidat. Quod adest memento

Componere aequus; cetera fluminis
Ritu feruntur, nunc medio alveo
  Cum pace delabentis Etruscum 35
    In mare, nunc lapides adesos

Stirpisque raptas et pecus et domos
Volventis una non sine montium
  Clamore vicinaeque silvae,
    Cum fera diluvies quietos 40

Irritat amnis. Ille potens sui
Laetusque deget, cui licet in diem
　Dixisse 'Vixi: cras vel atra
　　Nube polum pater occupato

Vel sole puro; non tamen inritum 45
Quodcumque retrost efficiet, neque
　Diffinget infectumque reddet
　　Quod fugiens semel hora vexit.'

Fortuna saevo laeta negotio et
Ludum insolentem ludere pertinax 50
　Transmutat incertos honores,
　　Nunc mihi nunc alii benigna.

Laudo manentem; si celeres quatit
Pennas, resigno quae dedit et mea
　Virtute me involvo probamque 55
　　Pauperiem sine dote quaero.

Non est meum, si mugiat Africis
Malus procellis, ad miseras preces
　Decurrere et votis pacisci,
　　Ne Cypriae Tyriaeque merces 60

Addant avaro divitias mari:
Tunc me biremis praesidio scaphae
　Tutum per Aegaeos tumultus
　　Aura feret geminusque Pollux.

XXX.

Exegi monumentum aere perennius
Regalique situ pyramidum altius,
Quod non imber edax, non Aquilo impotens
Possit diruere aut innumerabilis
Annorum series et fuga temporum. 5
Non omnis moriar, multaque pars mei
Vitabit Libitinam: usque ego postera
Crescam laude recens, dum Capitolium
Scandet cum tacita virgine pontifex.
Dicar, qua violens obstrepit Aufidus 10
Et qua pauper aquae Daunus agrestium
Regnavit populorum, ex humili potens
Princeps Aeolium carmen ad Italos
Deduxisse modos. Sume superbiam

Quaesitam meritis et mihi Delphica 15
Lauro cinge volens, Melpomene, comam.

CARMINUM

LIBER QUARTUS.

I.

Intermissa, Venus, diu
  Rursus bella moves? Parce, precor, precor.
Non sum qualis eram bonae
  Sub regno Cinarae. Desine, dulcium
Mater saeva Cupidinum, 5
  Circa lustra decem flectere mollibus
Iam durum imperiis: abi,
  Quo blandae iuvenum te revocant preces.
Tempestivius in domum
  Paulli, purpureis ales oloribus, 10
Comissabere Maximi,
  Si torrere iecur quaeris idoneum.
Namque et nobilis et decens
  Et pro sollicitis non tacitus reis
Et centum puer artium 15
  Late signa feret militiae tuae,
Et quandoque potentior
  Largi muneribus riserit aemuli,
Albanos prope te lacus
  Ponet marmoream sub trabe citrea. 20
Illic plurima naribus
  Duces tura, lyraeque et Berecyntiae
Delectabere tibiae
  Mixtis carminibus non sine fistula;
Illic bis pueri die 25
  Numen cum teneris virginibus tuum
Laudantes pede candido
  In morem Salium ter quatient humum.
Me nec femina nec puer
  Iam nec spes animi credula mutui, 30
Nec certare iuvat mero
  Nec vincire novis tempora floribus.
Sed cur heu, Ligurine, cur
  Manat rara meas lacrima per genas?
Cur facunda parum decoro 35

Inter verba cadit lingua silentio?
Nocturnis ego somniis
  Iam captum teneo, iam volucrem sequor
Te per gramina Martii
  Campi, te per aquas, dure, volubilis. 40

II.

Pindarum quisquis studet aemulari,
Iulle, ceratis ope Daedalea
Nititur pennis vitreo daturus
  Nomina ponto.

Monte decurrens velut amnis, imbres 5
Quem super notas aluere ripas,
Fervet immensusque ruit profundo
  Pindarus ore,

Laurea donandus Apollinari,
Seu per audacis nova dithyrambos 10
Verba devolvit numerisque fertur
  Lege solutis,

Seu deos regesve canit, deorum
Sanguinem, per quos cecidere iusta
Morte Centauri, cecidit tremendae 15
  Flamma Chimaerae,

Sive quos Elea domum reducit
Palma caelestis pugilemve equumve
Dicit et centum potiore signis
  Munere donat, 20

Flebili sponsae iuvenemve raptum
Plorat et viris animumque moresque
Aureos educit in astra nigroque
  Invidet Orco.

Multa Dircaeum levat aura cycnum, 25
Tendit, Antoni, quotiens in altos
Nubium tractus. Ego apis Matinae
  More modoque

Grata carpentis thyma per laborem
Plurimum circa nemus uvidique 30
Tiburis ripas operosa parvus
  Carmina fingo.

Concines maiore poeta plectro
Caesarem, quandoque trahet ferocis
Per sacrum clivum merita decorus 35
  Fronde Sygambros;

Quo nihil maius meliusve terris
Fata donavere bonique divi
Nec dabunt, quamvis redeant in aurum
  Tempora priscum. 40

Concines laetosque dies et urbis
Publicum ludum super impetrato
Fortis Augusti reditu forumque
  Litibus orbum.

Tum meae, si quid loquar audiendum, 45
Vocis accedet bona pars, et 'O Sol
Pulcher, o laudande!' canam recepto
  Caesare felix.

Teque dum procedis, 'Io Triumphe!'
Non semel dicemus, 'Io Triumphe!' 50
Civitas omnis dabimusque divis
  Tura benignis.

Te decem tauri totidemque vaccae,
Me tener solvet vitulus, relicta
Matre qui largis iuvenescit herbis 55
  In mea vota,

Fronte curvatos imitatus ignis
Tertium lunae referentis ortum,
Qua notam duxit, niveus videri,
  Cetera fulvus. 60

III.

Quem tu, Melpomene, semel
  Nascentem placido lumine videris,
Illum non labor Isthmius
  Clarabit pugilem, non equus impiger
Curru ducet Achaico
  Victorem, neque res bellica Deliis
Ornatmn foliis ducem,
  Quod regum tumidas contuderit minas,
Ostendet Capitolio;
  Sed quae Tibur aquae fertile praefluunt, 10

Et spissae nemorum comae
　　Fingent Aeolio carmine nobilem.
Romae principis urbium
　　Dignatur suboles inter amabilis
Vatum ponere me choros, 15
　　Et iam dente minus mordeor invido.
O testudinis aureae
　　Dulcem quae strepitum, Pieri, temperas,
O mutis quoque piscibus
　　Donatura cycni, si libeat, sonum, 20
Totum muneris hoc tuist,
　　Quod monstror digito praetereuntium
Romanae fidicen lyrae
　　Quod spiro et placeo, si placeo, tuumst.

IV.

Qualem ministrum fulminis alitem,
Cui rex deorum regnum in avis vagas
　　Permisit expertus fidelem
　　　Iuppiter in Ganymede flavo,

Olim iuventas et patrius vigor 5
Nido laborum propulit inscium,
　　Vernique iam nimbis remotis
　　　Insolitos docuere nisus

Venti paventem, mox in ovilia
Demisit hostem vividus impetus, 10
　　Nunc in reluctantis dracones
　　　Egit amor dapis atque pugnae;

Qualemve laetis caprea pascuis
Intenta fulvae matris ab ubere
　　Iam lacte depulsum leonem 15
　　　Dente novo peritura vidit:

Videre Raetis bella sub Alpibus
Drusum gerentem Vindelici; (quibus
　　Mos unde deductus per omne
　　　Tempus Amazonia securi 20

Dextras obarmet, quaerere distuli,
Nec scire fas est omnia); sed diu
　　Lateque victrices catervae
　　　Consiliis iuvenis revictae

Sensere quid mens rite, quid indoles 25
Nutrita faustis sub penetralibus
  Posset, quid Augusti paternus
    In pueros animus Nerones.

Fortes creantur fortibus et bonis;
Est in iuvencis, est in equis patrum 30
  Virtus, neque imbellem feroces
    Progenerant aquilae columbam;

Doctrina sed vim promovet insitam,
Rectique cultus pectora roborant;
  Utcumque defecere mores, 35
    Indecorant bene nata culpae.

Quid debeas, o Roma, Neronibus,
Testis Metaurum flumen et Hasdrubal
  Devictus et pulcher fugatis
    Ille dies Latio tenebris, 40

Qui primus alma risit adorea,
Dirus per urbis Afer ut Italas
  Ceu flamma per taedas vel Eurus
    Per Siculas equitavit undas.

Post hoc secundis usque laboribus 45
Romana pubes crevit, et impio
  Vastata Poenorum tumultu
    Fana deos habuere rectos,

Dixitque tandem perfidus Hannibal:
'Cervi luporum praeda rapacium, 50
  Sectamur ultro, quos opimus
    Fallere et effugerest triumphus.

Gens quae cremato fortis ab Ilio
Iactata Tuscis aequoribus sacra
  Natosque maturosque patres 55
    Pertulit Ausonias ad urbis,

Duris ut ilex tonsa bipennibus
Nigrae feraci frondis in Algido,
  Per damna, per caedis, ab ipso
    Ducit opes animumque ferro. 60

Non hydra secto corpore firmior
Vinci dolentem crevit in Herculem,
  Monstrumve submisere Colchi
    Maius Echioniaeve Thebae.

Merses profundo, pulchrior evenit; 65
Luctere, multa proruet integrum
  Cum laude victorem geretque
    Proelia coniugibus loquenda.

Carthagini iam non ego nuntios
Mittam superbos: occidit, occidit 70
  Spes omnis et fortuna nostri
    Nominis Hasdrubale interempto.'

Nil Claudiae non perficient manus,
Quas et benigno numine Iuppiter
  Defendit et curae sagaces 75
    Expediunt per acuta belli.

V.

Divis orte bonis, optime Romulae
Custos gentis, abes iam nimium diu;
Maturum reditum pollicitus patrum
  Sancto concilio redi.

Lucem redde tuae, dux bone, patriae: 5
Instar veris enim voltus ubi tuus
Adfulsit populo, gratior it dies
  Et soles melius nitent.

Ut mater iuvenem, quem Notus invido
Flatu Carpathii trans maris aequora 10
Cunctantem spatio longius annuo
  Dulci distinet a domo,

Votis ominibusque et precibus vocat,
Curvo nec faciem litore demovet,
Sic desideriis icta fidelibus 15
  Quaerit patria Caesarem.

Tutus bos etenim rura perambulat,
Nutrit rura Ceres almaque Faustitas,
Pacatum volitant per mare navitae,
  Culpari metuit fides, 20

Nullis polluitur casta domus stupris,
Mos et lex maculosum edomuit nefas,
Laudantur simili prole puerperae,
  Culpam poena premit comes.

Quis Parthum paveat, quis gelidum Scythen, 25
Quis Germania quos horrida parturit
Fetus incolumi Caesare? quis ferae
  Bellum curet Hiberiae?

Condit quisque diem collibus in suis,
Et vitem viduas ducit ad arbores; 30
Hinc ad vina redit laetus et alteris
  Te mensis adhibet deum;

Te multa prece, te prosequitur mero
Defuso pateris, et Laribus tuum
Miscet numen, uti Graecia Castoris 35
  Et magni memor Herculis.

'Longas o utinam, dux bone, ferias
Praestes Hesperiae!' dicimus integro
Sicci mane die, dicimus uvidi,
  Cum Sol Oceano subest. 40

VI.

Dive, quem proles Niobea magnae
Vindicem linguae Tityosque raptor
Sensit et Troiae prope victor altae
  Phthius Achilles,

Ceteris maior, tibi miles impar, 5
Filius quamvis Thetidis marinae
Dardanas turris quateret tremenda
  Cuspide pugnax.

Ille mordaci velut icta ferro
Pinus aut impulsa cupressus Euro, 10
Procidit late posuitque collum in
  Pulvere Teucro.

Ille non inclusus equo Minervae
Sacra mentito male feriatos
Troas et laetam Priami choreis 15
  Falleret aulam;

Sed palam captis gravis, heu nefas, heu,
Nescios fari pueros Achivis
Ureret flammis, etiam latentem
  Matris in alvo, 20

Ni tuis victus Venerisque gratae
Vocibus divum pater adnuisset
Rebus Aeneae potiore ductos
　Alite muros.

Doctor Argivae fidicen Thaliae, 25
Phoebe, qui Xantho lavis amne crinis,
Dauniae defende decus Camenae,
　Levis Agyieu.

Spiritum Phoebus mihi, Phoebus artem
Carminis nomenque dedit poetae. 30
Virginum primae puerique claris
　Patribus orti,

Deliae tutela deae, fugacis
Lyncas et cervos cohibentis arcu,
Lesbium servate pedem meique 35
　Pollicis ictum,

Rite Latonae puerum canentes,
Rite crescentem face Noctilucam,
Prosperam frugum celeremque pronos
　Volvere mensis. 40

Nupta iam dices 'Ego dis amicum,
Saeculo festas referente luces,
Reddidi carmen docilis modorum
　Vatis Horati.'

VII.

Diffugere nives, redeunt iam gramina campis
　Arboribusque comae;
Mutat terra vices et decrescentia ripas
　Flumina praetereunt;
Gratia cum Nymphis geminisque sororibus audet 5
　Ducere nuda choros.
Immortalia ne speres, monet annus et almum
　Quae rapit hora diem.
Frigora mitescunt Zephyris, ver proterit aestas
　Interitura simul 10
Pomifer autumnus fruges effuderit, et mox
　Bruma recurrit iners.
Damna tamen celeres reparant caelestia lunae:
　Nos ubi decidimus
Quo pater Aeneas, quo dives Tullus et Ancus, 15

Pulvis et umbra sumus.
Quis scit an adiciant hodiernae crastina summae
  Tempora di superi?
Cuncta manus avidas fugient heredis, amico
  Quae dederis animo. 20
Cum semel occideris et de te splendida Minos
  Fecerit arbitria,
Non, Torquate, genus, non te facundia, non te
  Restituet pietas.
Infernis neque enim tenebris Diana pudicum 25
  Liberat Hippolytum,
Nec Lethaea valet Theseus abrumpere caro
  Vincula Pirithoo.

VII.

Donarem pateras grataque commodus,
Censorine, meis aera sodalibus,
Donarem tripodas, praemia fortium
Graiorum, neque tu pessima munerum
Ferres, divite me scilicet artium, 5
Quas aut Parrhasius protulit aut Scopas,
Hic saxo, liquidis ille coloribus
Sollers nunc hominem ponere, nunc deum.
Sed non haec mihi vis, nec tibi talium
Res est aut animus deliciarum egens. 10
Gaudes carminibus; carmina possumus
Donare et pretium dicere muneris.
Non incisa notis marmora publicis,
Per quae spiritus et vita redit bonis
Post mortem ducibus, non celeres fugae 15
Reiectaeque retrorsum Hannibalis minae,
Non incendia Carthaginis impiae
Eius, qui domita nomen ab Africa
Lucratus rediit, clarius indicant
Laudes quam Calabrae Pierides; neque 20
Si chartae sileant quod bene feceris
Mercedem tuleris. Quid foret Iliae
Mavortisque puer, si taciturnitas
Obstaret meritis invida Romuli?
Ereptum Stygiis fluctibus Aeacum 25
Virtus et favor et lingua potentium
Vatum divitibus consecrat insulis.
Dignum laude virum Musa vetat mori:
Caelo Musa beat. Sic Iovis interest
Optatis epulis impiger Hercules, 30
Clarum Tyndaridae sidus ab infimis

Quassas eripiunt aequoribus ratis,
Ornatus viridi tempora pampino
Liber vota bonos ducit ad exitus.

IX.

Ne forte credas interitura quae
Longe sonantem natus ad Aufidum
  Non ante volgatas per artis
    Verba loquor socianda chordis:

Non, si priores Maeonius tenet 5
Sedes Homerus, Pindaricae latent
  Ceaeque et Alcaei minaces
    Stesichorique graves Camenae;

Nec si quid olim lusit Anacreon
Delevit aetas; spirat adhuc amor 10
  Vivuntque commissi calores
    Aeoliae fidibus puellae.

Non sola comptos arsit adulteri
Crinis et aurum vestibus illitum
  Mirata regalisque cultus 15
    Et comites Helene Lacaena,

Primusve Teucer tela Cydonio
Direxit arcu; non semel Ilios
  Vexata; non pugnavit ingens
    Idomeneus Sthenelusve solus 20

Dicenda Musis proelia; non ferox
Hector vel acer Deiphobus gravis
  Excepit ictus pro pudicis
    Coniugibus puerisque primus.

Vixere fortes ante Agamemnona 25
Multi; sed omnes inlacrimabiles
  Urgentur ignotique longa
    Nocte, carent quia vate sacro.

Paullum sepultae distat inertiae
Celata virtus. Non ego te meis 30
  Chartis inornatum silebo,
    Totve tuos patiar labores

Impune, Lolli, carpere lividas
Obliviones. Est animus tibi
  Rerumque prudens et secundis 35
    Temporibus dubiisque rectus,

Vindex avarae fraudis et abstinens
Ducentis ad se cuncta pecuniae,
  Consulque non unius anni,
    Sed quotiens bonus atque fidus 40

Iudex honestum praetulit utili,
Reiecit alto dona nocentium
  Voltu, per obstantis catervas
    Explicuit sua victor arma.

Non possidentem multa vocaveris 45
Recte beatum; rectius occupat
  Nomen beati, qui deorum
    Muneribus sapienter uti

Duramque callet pauperiem pati
Peiusque leto flagitium timet, 50
  Non ille pro caris amicis
    Aut patria timidus perire.

X.

O crudelis adhuc et Veneris muneribus potens,
Insperata tuae cum veniet pluma superbiae
Et, quae nunc umeris involitant, deciderint comae,
Nunc et qui color est puniceae flore prior rosae
Mutatus Ligurinum in faciem verterit hispidam, 5
Dices 'Heu,' quotiens te speculo videris alterum,
'Quae mens est hodie, cur eadem non puero fuit,
Vel cur his animis incolumes non redeunt genae?'

XI.

Est mihi nonum superantis annum
Plenus Albani cadus; est in horto,
Phylli, nectendis apium coronis;
  Est hederae vis

Multa, qua crinis religata fulges; 5
Ridet argento domus; ara castis
Vincta verbenis avet immolato
    Spargier agno;

Cuncta festinat manus, huc et illuc
Cursitant mixtae pueris puellae; 10
Sordidum flammae trepidant rotantes
    Vertice fumum.

Ut tamen noris quibus advoceris
Gaudiis, Idus tibi sunt agendae,
Qui dies mensem Veneris marinae 15
    Findit Aprilem,   ˜

Iure sollemnis mihi sanctiorque
Paene natali proprio, quod ex hac
Luce Maecenas meus adfluentis
    Ordinat annos. 20

Telephum, quem tu petis, occupavit
Non tuae sortis iuvenem puella
Dives et lasciva, tenetque grata
    Compede vinctum.

Terret ambustus Phaethon avaras 25
Spes, et exemplum grave praebet ales
Pegasus terrenum equitem gravatus
    Bellerophonten,

Semper ut te digna sequare et ultra
Quam licet sperare nefas putando 30
Disparem vites. Age iam, meorum
    Finis amorum,

(Non enim posthac alia calebo
Femina) condisce modos, amanda
Voce quos reddas: minuentur atrae 35
    Carmine curae.

XII.

Iam veris comites, quae mare temperant,
Impellunt animae lintea Thraciae;
Iam nec prata rigent nec fluvii strepunt
    Hiberna nive turgidi.

Nidum ponit, Ityn flebiliter gemens, 5
Infelix avis et Cecropiae domus
Aeternum opprobrium, quod male barbaras
  Regumst ulta libidines.

Dicunt in tenero gramine pinguium
Custodes ovium carmina fistula 10
Delectantque deum cui pecus et nigri
  Colles Arcadiae placent.

Adduxere sitim tempora, Vergili;
Sed pressum Calibus ducere Liberum
Si gestis, iuvenum nobilium cliens, 15
  Nardo vina mereberis.

Nardi parvus onyx eliciet cadum,
Qui nunc Sulpiciis accubat horreis,
Spes donare novas largus amaraque
  Curarum eluere efficax. 20

Ad quae si properas gaudia, cum tua
Velox merce veni: non ego te meis
Immunem meditor tinguere poculis,
  Plena dives ut in domo.

Verum pone moras et studium lucri, 25
Nigrorumque memor, dum licet, ignium
Misce stultitiam consiliis brevem:
  Dulcest desipere in loco.

XIII.

Audivere, Lyce, di mea vota, di
Audivere, Lyce: fis anus, et tamen
  Vis formosa videri,
    Ludisque et bibis impudens

Et cantu tremulo pota Cupidinem 5
Lentum sollicitas. Ille virentis et
  Doctae psallere Chiae
    Pulchris excubat in genis.

Importunus enim transvolat aridas
Quercus et refugit te, quia luridi 10
  Dentes te, quia rugae
    Turpant et capitis nives.

Nec Coae referunt iam tibi purpurae
Nec cari lapides tempora, quae semel
  Notis condita fastis 15
    Inclusit volucris dies.

Quo fugit venus, heu, quove color? decens
Quo motus? Quid habes illius, illius,
  Quae spirabat amores,
    Quae me surpuerat mihi, 20

Felix post Cinaram notaque et artium
Gratarum facies? Sed Cinarae brevis
  Annos fata dederunt,
    Servatura diu parem

Cornicis vetulae temporibus Lycen, 25
Possent ut iuvenes visere fervidi
  Multo non sine risu
    Dilapsam in cineres facem.

XIV.

Quae cura patrum quaeve Quiritium
Plenis honorum muneribus tuas,
  Auguste, virtutes in aevum
    Per titulos memoresque fastos

Aeternet, o qua sol habitabilis 5
Inlustrat oras, maxime principum?
  Quem legis expertes Latinae
    Vindelici didicere nuper

Quid marte posses. Milite nam tuo
Drusus Genaunos, implacidum genus, 10
  Breunosque velocis et arcis
    Alpibus impositas tremendis

Deiecit acer plus vice simplici;
Maior Neronum mox grave proelium
Commisit immanisque Raetos 15
  Auspiciis pepulit secundis,

Spectandus in certamine Martio,
Devota morti pectora liberae
  Quantis fatigaret ruinis,
    Indomitas prope qualis undas 20

Exercet Auster, Pleiadum choro
Scindente nubis, impiger hostium
  Vexare turmas et frementem
    Mittere equum medios per ignis.

Sic tauriformis volvitur Aufidus, 25
Qui regna Dauni praefluit Apuli,
  Cum saevit horrendamque cultis
    Diluviem meditatur agris,

Ut barbarorum Claudius agmina
Ferrata vasto diruit impetu 30
  Primosque et extremos metendo
    Stravit humum sine clade victor,

Te copias, te consilium et tuos
Praebente divos. Nam tibi, quo die
  Portus Alexandrea supplex 35
    Et vacuam patefecit aulam,

Fortuna lustro prospera tertio
Belli secundos reddidit exitus,
  Laudemque et optatum peractis
    Imperiis decus adrogavit. 40

Te Cantaber non ante domabilis
Medusque et Indus, te profugus Scythes
  Miratur, o tutela praesens
    Italiae dominaeque Romae.

Te fontium qui celat origines 45
Nilusque et Hister, te rapidus Tigris,
  Te beluosus qui remotis
    Obstrepit Oceanus Britannis,

Te non paventis funera Galliae
Duraeque tellus audit Hiberiae, 50
  Te caede gaudentes Sygambri
    Compositis venerantur armis.

XV.

Phoebus volentem proelia me loqui
Victas et urbis increpuit lyra,
  Ne parva Tyrrhenum per aequor
    Vela darem. Tua, Caesar, aetas

Fruges et agris rettulit uberes 5
Et signa nostro restituit Iovi
  Derepta Parthorum superbis
    Postibus et vacuum duellis

Ianum Quirini clausit et ordinem
Rectum evaganti frena licentiae 10
  Iniecit emovitque culpas
    Et veteres revocavit artis,

Per quas Latinum nomen et Italae
Crevere vires famaque et imperi
  Porrecta maiestas ad ortus 15
    Solis ab Hesperio cubili.

Custode rerum Caesare non furor
Civilis aut vis exiget otium,
  Non ira, quae procudit ensis
    Et miseras inimicat urbis. 20

Non qui profundum Danuvium bibunt
Edicta rumpent Iulia, non Getae,
  Non Seres infidive Persae,
    Non Tanain prope flumen orti.

Nosque et profestis lucibus et sacris 25
Inter iocosi munera Liberi
  Cum prole matronisque nostris,
    Rite deos prius adprecati,

Virtute functos more patrum duces
Lydis remixto carmine tibiis 30
  Troiamque et Anchisen et almae
    Progeniem Veneris canemus.

CARMEN

SAECULARE.

Phoebe silvarumque potens Diana,
Lucidum caeli decus, o colendi
Semper et culti, date quae precamur
  Tempore sacro,

Quo Sibyllini monuere versus 5
Virgines lectas puerosque castos
Dis quibus septem placuere colles
  Dicere carmen.

Alme Sol, curru nitido diem qui
Promis et celas aliusque et idem 10
Nasceris, possis nihil urbe Roma
  Visere maius!

Rite maturos aperire partus
Lenis, Ilithyia, tuere matres,
Sive tu Lucina probas vocari 15
  Seu Genitalis:

Diva, producas subolem patrumque
Prosperes decreta super iugandis
Feminis prolisque novae feraci
  Lege marita, 20

Certus undenos deciens per annos
Orbis ut cantus referatque ludos
Ter die claro totiensque grata
  Nocte frequentis.

Vosque veraces cecinisse, Parcae, 25
Quod semel dictumst stabilisque rerum
Terminus servet, bona iam peractis
  Iungite fata.

Fertilis frugum pecorisque tellus
Spicea donet Cererem corona; 30
Nutriant fetus et aquae salubres
  Et Iovis aurae.

Condito mitis placidusque telo
Supplices audi pueros, Apollo;
Siderum regina bicornis, audi, 35
  Luna, puellas:

Roma si vestrumst opus, Iliaeque
Litus Etruscum tenuere turmae,
Iussa pars mutare Laris et urbem
  Sospite cursu, 40

Cui per ardentem sine fraude Troiam
Castus Aeneas patriae superstes
Liberum munivit iter, daturus
  Plura relictis:

Di, probos mores docili iuventae, 45
Di, senectuti placidae quietem,
Romulae genti date remque prolemque
  Et decus omne.

Quaeque vos bobus veneratur albis
Clarus Anchisae Venerisque sanguis, 50
Impetret, bellante prior, iacentem
  Lenis in hostem.

Iam mari terraque manus potentis
Medus Albanasque timet securis,
Iam Scythae responsa petunt superbi 55
  Nuper, et Indi.

Iam Fides et Pax et Honor Pudorque
Priscus et neglecta redire Virtus
Audet, adparetque beata pleno
  Copia cornu. 60

Augur et fulgente decorus arcu
Phoebus acceptusque novem Camenis,
Qui salutari levat arte fessos
  Corporis artus,

Si Palatinas videt aequus aras, 65
Remque Romanam Latiumque felix
Alterum in lustrum meliusque semper
  Prorogat aevum.

Quaeque Aventinum tenet Algidumque,
Quindecim Diana preces virorum 70
Curat et votis puerorum amicas
  Adplicat auris.

Haec Iovem sentire deosque cunctos
Spem bonam certamque domum reporto,
Doctus et Phoebi chorus et Dianae 75
  Dicere laudes.

EPODON

LIBER.

I.

Ibis Liburnis inter alta navium,
  Amice, propugnacula,
Paratus omne Caesaris periculum
  Subire, Maecenas, tuo.
Quid nos, quibus te vita si superstite 5
  Iucunda, si contra, gravis?
Utrumne iussi persequemur otium
  Non dulce, ni tecum simul,
An hunc laborem mente laturi, decet
  Qua ferre non mollis viros? 10
Feremus, et te vel per Alpium iuga
  Inhospitalem et Caucasum
Vel Occidentis usque ad ultimum sinum
  Forti sequemur pectore.
Roges tuum labore quid iuvem meo, 15
  Imbellis ac firmus parum?
Comes minore sum futurus in metu,
  Qui maior absentis habet:
Ut adsidens implumibus pullis avis
  Serpentium adlapsus timet 20
Magis relictis, non, ut adsit, auxili
  Latura plus praesentibus.
Libenter hoc et omne militabitur
  Bellum in tuae spem gratiae,
Non ut iuvencis inligata pluribus 25
  Aratra nitantur meis
Pecusve Calabris ante sidus fervidum
  Lucana mutet pascuis,
Nec ut superni villa candens Tusculi
  Circaea tangat moenia. 30
Satis superque me benignitas tua
  Ditavit: haud paravero,
Quod aut avarus ut Chremes terra premam,
  Discinctus aut perdam nepos.

II.

'Beatus ille qui procul negotiis,
  Ut prisca gens mortalium,
Paterna rura bobus exercet suis,
  Solutus omni faenore,
Neque excitatur classico miles truci, 5
  Neque horret iratum mare,
Forumque vitat et superba civium
  Potentiorum limina.

Ergo aut adulta vitium propagine
  Altas maritat populos, 10
Aut in reducta valle mugientium
  Prospectat errantis greges,
Inutilisve falce ramos amputans
  Feliciores inserit,
Aut pressa puris mella condit amphoris, 15
  Aut tondet infirmas ovis;
Vel, cum decorum mitibus pomis caput
  Autumnus agris extulit,
Ut gaudet insitiva decerpens pira
  Certantem et uvam purpurae, 20
Qua muneretur te, Priape, et te, pater
  Silvane, tutor finium.
Libet iacere modo sub antiqua ilice,
  Modo in tenaci gramine.
Labuntur altis interim ripis aquae, 25
  Queruntur in silvis aves,
Fontesque lymphis obstrepunt manantibus,
  Somnos quod invitet levis.
At cum tonantis annus hibernus Iovis
  Imbris nivisque comparat, 30
Aut trudit acris hinc et hinc multa cane
  Apros in obstantis plagas,
Aut amite levi rara tendit retia,
  Turdis edacibus dolos,
Pavidumque leporem et advenam laqueo gruem 35
  Iucunda captat praemia.
Quis non malarum, quas amor curas habet,
  Haec inter obliviscitur?
Quod si pudica mulier in partem iuvet
  Domum atque dulcis liberos, 40
Sabina qualis aut perusta solibus
  Pernicis uxor Apuli,
Sacrum vetustis exstruat lignis focum
  Lassi sub adventum viri,
Claudensque textis cratibus laetum pecus 45
  Distenta siccet ubera,
Et horna dulci vina promens dolio
  Dapes inemptas adparet:
Non me Lucrina iuverint conchylia
  Magisve rhombus aut scari, 50
Si quos Eois intonata fluctibus
  Hiems ad hoc vertat mare;
Non Afra avis descendat in ventrem meum,
  Non attagen Ionicus
Iucundior, quam lecta de pinguissimis 55
  Oliva ramis arborum
Aut herba lapathi prata amantis et gravi
  Malvae salubres corpori,

Vel agna festis caesa Terminalibus
  Vel haedus ereptus lupo. 60
Has inter epulas ut iuvat pastas ovis
  Videre properantis domum,
Videre fessos vomerem inversum boves
  Collo trahentis languido,
Positosque vernas, ditis examen domus, 65
  Circum renidentis Laris.'
Haec ubi locutus faenerator Alfius,
  Iam iam futurus rusticus,
Omnem redegit Idibus pecuniam,
  Quaerit Kalendis ponere. 70

III.

Parentis olim si quis impia manu
  Senile guttur fregerit,
Edit cicutis allium nocentius.
  O dura messorum ilia!
Quid hoc veneni saevit in praecordiis? 5
  Num viperinus his cruor
Incoctus herbis me fefellit? an malas
  Canidia tractavit dapes?
Ut Argonautas praeter omnis candidum
  Medea miratast ducem, 10
Ignota tauris inligaturum iuga
  Perunxit hoc Iasonem;
Hoc delibutis ulta donis paelicem,
  Serpente fugit alite.
Nec tantus umquam siderum insedit vapor 15
  Siticulosae Apuliae,
Nec munus umeris efficacis Herculis
  Inarsit aestuosius.
At si quid umquam tale concupiveris,
  Iocose Maecenas, precor 20
Manum puella savio opponat tuo,
  Extrema et in sponda cubet.

IV.

Lupis et agnis quanta sortito obtigit
  Tecum mihi discordiast,
Hibericis peruste funibus latus
  Et crura dura compede.

Licet superbus ambules pecunia, 5
  Fortuna non mutat genus.
Videsne, Sacram metiente te viam
  Cum bis trium ulnarum toga,
Ut ora vertat huc et huc euntium
  Liberrima indignatio? 10
'Sectus flagellis hic triumviralibus
  Praeconis ad fastidium
Arat Falerni mille fundi iugera,
  Et Appiam mannis terit,
Sedilibusque magnus in primis eques 15
  Othone contempto sedet.
Quid attinet tot ora navium gravi
  Rostrata duci pondere
Contra latrones atque servilem manum,
  Hoc, hoc tribuno militum?' 20

V.

'At, o deorum quidquid in caelo regit
  Terras et humanum genus,
Quid iste fert tumultus et quid omnium
  Voltus in unum me truces?
Per liberos te, si vocata partubus 5
  Lucina veris adfuit,
Per hoc inane purpurae decus precor,
  Per improbaturum haec Iovem,
Quid ut noverca me intueris aut uti
  Petita ferro belua?' 10
Ut haec trementi questus ore constitit
  Insignibus raptis puer,
Impube corpus, quale posset impia
  Mollire Thracum pectora;
Canidia, brevibus implicata viperis 15
  Crinis et incomptum caput,
Iubet sepulcris caprificos erutas,
  Iubet cupressus funebris
Et uncta turpis ova ranae sanguine
  Plumamque nocturnae strigis 20
Herbasque quas Iolcos atque Hiberia
  Mittit venenorum ferax,
Et ossa ab ore rapta ieiunae canis
  Flammis aduri Colchicis.
At expedita Sagana, per totam domum 25
  Spargens Avernalis aquas,
Horret capillis ut marinus asperis
  Echinus ant currens aper.

Abacta nulla Veia conscientia
  Ligonibus duris humum 30
Exhauriebat, ingemens laboribus,
  Quo posset infossus puer
Longo die bis terque mutatae dapis
  Inemori spectaculo,
Cum promineret ore, quantum exstant aqua 35
  Suspensa mento corpora:
Exsecta uti medulla et aridum iecur
  Amoris esset poculum,
Interminato cum semel fixae cibo
  Intabuissent pupulae. 40
Non defuisse masculae libidinis
  Ariminensem Foliam
Et otiosa credidit Neapolis
  Et omne vicinum oppidum,
Quae sidera excantata voce Thessala 45
  Lunamque caelo deripit.
Hic inresectum saeva dente livido
  Canidia rodens pollicem,
Quid dixit aut quid tacuit? 'O rebus meis
  Non infideles arbitrae, 50
Nox et Diana, quae silentium regis,
  Arcana cum fiunt sacra,
Nunc nunc adeste, nunc in hostilis domos
  Iram atque numen vertite.
Formidolosis dum latent silvis ferae 55
  Dulci sopore languidae,
Senem, quod omnes rideant, adulterum
  Latrent Suburanae canes,
Nardo perunctum, quale non perfectius
  Meae laborarint manus. 60
Quid accidit? Cur dira barbarae minus
  Venena Medeae valent,
Quibus superbam fugit ulta paelicem,
  Magni Creontis filiam,
Cum palla, tabo munus imbutum, novam 65
  Incendio nuptam abstulit?
Atqui nec herba nec latens in asperis
  Radix fefellit me locis.
Indormit unctis omnium cubilibus
  Oblivione paelicum. 70
A, a, solutus ambulat veneficae
  Scientioris carmine!
Non usitatis, Vare, potionibus,
  O multa fleturum caput,
Ad me recurres, nec vocata mens tua 75
  Marsis redibit vocibus.
Maius parabo, maius infundam tibi
  Fastidienti poculum,

Priusque caelum sidet inferius mari
　　Tellure porrecta super, 80
Quam non amore sic meo flagres uti
　　Bitumen atris ignibus.'
Sub haec puer iam non, ut ante, mollibus,
　　Lenire verbis impias,
Sed dubius unde rumperet silentium, 85
　　Misit Thyesteas preces:
'Venena magnum fas nefasque non valent
　　Convertere humanam vicem.
Diris agam vos; dira detestatio
　　Nulla expiatur victima. 90
Quin, ubi perire iussus exspiravero,
　　Nocturnus occurram Furor,
Petamque voltus umbra curvis unguibus,
　　Quae vis deorumst Manium,
Et inquietis adsidens praecordiis 95
　　Pavore somnos auferam.
Vos turba vicatim hinc et hinc saxis petens
　　Contundet obscenas anus;
Post insepulta membra different lupi
　　Et Esquilinae alites, 100
Neque hoc parentes, heu mihi superstites,
　　Effugerit spectaculum.'

VI.

Quid immerentis hospites vexas, canis
　　Ignavus adversum lupos?
Quin huc inanis, si potes, vertis minas,
　　Et me remorsurum petis?
Nam qualis aut Molossus aut fulvus Lacon, 5
　　Amica vis pastoribus,
Agam per altas aure sublata nivis,
　　Quaecumque praecedet fera;
Tu, cum timenda voce complesti nemus,
　　Proiectum odoraris cibum. 10
Cave, cave: namque in malos asperrimus
　　Parata tollo cornua,
Qualis Lycambae spretus infido gener,
　　Aut acer hostis Bupalo.
An, si quis atro dente me petiverit, 15
　　Inultus ut flebo puer?

VII.

Quo, quo scelesti ruitis? aut cur dexteris
   Aptantur enses conditi?
Parumne campis atque Neptuno super
   Fusumst Latini sanguinis,
Non ut superbas invidae Carthaginis 5
   Romanus arcis ureret,
Intactus aut Britannus ut descenderet
   Sacra catenatus via,
Sed ut secundum vota Parthorum sua
   Urbs haec periret dextera? 10
Neque hic lupis mos nec fuit leonibus
   Umquam nisi in dispar feris.
Furorne caecus an rapit vis acrior
   An culpa? Responsum date!
Tacent, et albus ora pallor inficit, 15
   Mentesque perculsae stupent.
Sic est: acerba fata Romanos agunt
   Scelusque fraternae necis,
Ut immerentis fluxit in terram Remi
   Sacer nepotibus cruor. 20

IX.

Quando repostum Caecubum ad festas dapes,
   Victore laetus Caesare,
Tecum sub alta—sic Iovi gratum—domo,
   Beate Maecenas, bibam,
Sonante mixtum tibiis carmen lyra, 5
   Hac Dorium, illis barbarum?
Ut nuper, actus cum freto Neptunius
   Dux fugit ustis navibus,
Minatus Urbi vincla, quae detraxerat
   Servis amicus perfidis. 10
Romanus eheu—posteri negabitis—
   Emancipatus feminae
Fert vallum et arma miles et spadonibus
   Servire rugosis potest,
Interque signa turpe militaria 15
   Sol adspicit conopium.
Ad hunc frementis verterunt bis mille equos
   Galli, canentes Caesarem,
Hostiliumque navium portu latent
   Puppes sinistrorsum citae. 20
Io Triumphe, tu moraris aureos
   Currus et intactas boves?

Io Triumphe, nec Iugurthino parem
  Bello reportasti ducem,
Neque Africanum, cui super Carthaginem 25
  Virtus sepulcrum condidit.
Terra marique victus hostis punico
  Lugubre mutavit sagum.
Aut ille centum nobilem Cretam urbibus,
  Ventis iturus non suis, 30
Exercitatas aut petit Syrtis Noto,
  Aut fertur incerto mari.
Capaciores adfer huc, puer, scyphos
  Et Chia vina aut Lesbia,
Vel quod fluentem nauseam coerceat 35
  Metire nobis Caecubum.
Curam metumque Caesaris rerum iuvat
  Dulci Lyaeo solvere.

X.

Mala soluta navis exit alite,
  Ferens olentem Mevium:
Ut horridis utrumque verberes latus,
  Auster, memento fluctibus.
Niger rudentis Eurus inverso mari 5
  Fractosque remos differat;
Insurgat Aquilo, quantus altis montibus
  Frangit trementis ilices;
Nec sidus atra nocte amicum adpareat,
  Qua tristis Orion cadit; 10
Quietiore nec feratur aequore,
  Quam Graia victorum manus,
Cum Pallas usto vertit iram ab Ilio
  In impiam Aiacis ratem.
O quantus instat navitis sudor tuis 15
  Tibique pallor luteus
Et illa non virilis eiulatio
  Preces et aversum ad Iovem,
Ionius udo cum remugiens sinus
  Noto carinam ruperit. 20
Opima quod si praeda curvo litore
  Porrecta mergos iuverit,
Libidinosus immolabitur caper
  Et agna Tempestatibus.

XIII.

Horrida tempestas caelum contraxit, et imbres
  Nivesque deducunt Iovem; nunc mare, nunc siluae
Threicio Aquilone sonant. Rapiamus, amice,
  Occasionem de die, dumque virent genua
Et decet, obducta solvatur fronte senectus. 5
  Tu vina Torquato move consule pressa meo.
Cetera mitte loqui: deus haec fortasse benigna
  Reducet in sedem vice. Nunc et Achaemenio
Perfundi nardo iuvat et fide Cyllenea
  Levare diris pectora sollicitudinibus, 10
Nobilis ut grandi cecinit Centaurus alumno:
  'Invicte, mortalis dea nate puer Thetide,
Te manet Assaraci tellus, quam frigida parvi
  Findunt Scamandri flumina lubricus et Simois,
Unde tibi reditum certo subtemine Parcae 15
  Rupere, nec mater domum caerula te revehet.
Illic omne malum vino cantuque levato,
  Deformis aegrimoniae dulcibus adloquiis.'

XIV.

Mollis inertia cur tantam diffuderit imis
  Oblivionem sensibus,
Pocula Lethaeos ut si ducentia somnos
  Arente fauce traxerim,
Candide Maecenas, occidis saepe rogando: 5
  Deus, deus nam me vetat
Inceptos, olim promissum carmen, iambos
  Ad umbilicum adducere.
Non aliter Samio dicunt arsisse Bathyllo
  Anacreonta Teium, 10
Qui persaepe cava testudine flevit amorem
  Non elaboratum ad pedem.
Ureris ipse miser: quod si non pulchrior ignis
  Accendit obsessam Ilion,
Gaude sorte tua; me libertina nec uno 15
  Contenta Phryne macerat.

XV.

Nox erat et caelo fulgebat Luna sereno
  Inter minora sidera,

Cum tu, magnorum numen laesura deorum,
  In verba iurabas mea,
Artius atque hedera procera adstringitur ilex, 5
  Lentis adhaerens bracchiis,
Dum pecori lupus et nautis infestus Orion
  Turbaret hibernum mare,
Intonsosque agitaret Apollinis aura capillos,
  Fore hunc amorem mutuum. 10
O dolitura mea multum virtute Neaera!
  Nam si quid in Flacco virist,
Non feret adsiduas potiori te dare noctis,
  Et quaeret iratus parem:
Nec semel offensi cedet constantia formae, 15
  Si certus intrarit dolor.
Et tu, quicumque's felicior atque meo nunc
  Superbus incedis malo,
Sis pecore et multa dives tellure licebit
  Tibique Pactolus fluat, 20
Nec te Pythagorae fallant arcana renati,
  Formaque vincas Nirea,
Eheu, translatos alio maerebis amores;
  Ast ego vicissim risero.

XVI.

Altera iam teritur bellis civilibus aetas,
  Suis et ipsa Roma viribus ruit.
Quam neque finitimi valuerunt perdere Marsi
  Minacis aut Etrusca Porsenae manus
Aemula nec virtus Capuae nec Spartacus acer 5
  Novisque rebus infidelis Allobrox,
Nec fera caerulea domuit Germania pube
  Parentibusque abominatus Hannibal,
Impia perdemus devoti sanguinis aetas,
  Ferisque rursus occupabitur solum. 10
Barbarus heu cineres insistet victor et urbem
  Eques sonante verberabit ungula,
Quaeque carent ventis et solibus ossa Quirini,
  Nefas videre! dissipabit insolens.
Forte, quid expediat, communiter aut melior pars 15
  Malis carere quaeritis laboribus.
Nulla sit hac potior sententia: Phocaeorum
  Velut profugit exsecrata civitas
Agros atque Laris patrios habitandaque fana
  Apris reliquit et rapacibus lupis, 20
Ire, pedes quocumque ferent, quocumque per undas
  Notus vocabit aut protervus Africus.

Sic placet? an melius quis habet suadere? Secunda
 Ratem occupare quid moramur alite?
Sed iuremus in haec: 'Simul imis saxa renarint 25
 Vadis levata, ne redire sit nefas,
Neu conversa domum pigeat dare lintea, quando
 Padus Matina laverit cacumina,
In mare seu celsus procurrerit Appenninus,
 Novaque monstra iunxerit libidine 30
Mirus amor, iuvet ut tigris subsidere cervis,
 Adulteretur et columba miluo,
Credula nec ravos timeant armenta leones,
 Ametque salsa levis hircus aequora.'
Haec et quae poterunt reditus abscindere dulcis 35
 Eamus omnis exsecrata civitas,
Aut pars indocili melior grege; mollis et exspes
 Inominata perprimat cubilia.
Vos, quibus est virtus, muliebrem tollite luctum,
 Etrusca praeter et volate litora. 40
Nos manet Oceanus circumvagus; arva beata
 Petamus, arva divites et insulas,
Reddit ubi cererem tellus inarata quotannis
 Et imputata floret usque vinea,
Germinat et numquam fallentis termes olivae, 45
 Suamque pulla ficus ornat arborem,
Mella cava manant ex ilice, montibus altis
 Levis crepante lympha desilit pede.
Illic iniussae veniunt ad mulctra capellae,
 Refertque tenta grex amicus ubera, 50
Nec vespertinus circumgemit ursus ovile,
 Nec intumescit alta viperis humus.
Pluraque felices mirabimur, ut neque largis
 Aquosus Eurus arva radat imbribus,
Pinguia nec siccis urantur semina glaebis, 55
 Utrumque rege temperante caelitum.
Non huc Argoo contendit remige pinus,
 Neque impudica Colchis intulit pedem;
Non huc Sidonii torserunt cornua nautae,
 Laboriosa nec cohors Ulixei. 60
Nulla nocent pecori contagia, nullius astri
 Gregem aestuosa torret impotentia.
Iuppiter illa piae secrevit litora genti,
 Ut inquinavit aere tempus aureum;
Aere, dehinc ferro duravit saecula, quorum 65
 Piis secunda vate me datur fuga.

XVII.

'Iam iam efficaci do manus scientiae,
Supplex et oro regna per Proserpinae,
Per et Dianae non movenda numina,
Per atque libros carminum valentium
Refixa caelo devocare sidera, 5
Canidia, parce vocibus tandem sacris
Citumque retro solve, solve turbinem!
Movit nepotem Telephus Nereium,
In quem superbus ordinarat agmina
Mysorum et in quem tela acuta torserat. 10
Unxere matres Iliae addictum feris
Alitibus atque canibus homicidam Hectorem,
Postquam relictis moenibus rex procidit
Heu pervicacis ad pedes Achillei.
Saetosa duris exuere pellibus 15
Laboriosi remiges Ulixei
Volente Circa membra; tunc mens et sonus
Relapsus atque notus in voltus honor.
Dedi satis superque poenarum tibi,
Amata nautis multum et institoribus. 20
Fugit iuventas et verecundus color
Reliquit ossa pelle amicta lurida,
Tuis capillus albus est odoribus;
Nullum ab labore me reclinat otium;
Urget diem nox et dies noctem, nequest 25
Levare tenta spiritu praecordia.
Ergo negatum vincor ut credam miser,
Sabella pectus increpare carmina
Caputque Marsa dissilire nenia.
Quid amplius vis? O mare et terra, ardeo, 30
Quantum neque atro delibutus Hercules
Nessi cruore, nec Sicana fervida
Virens in Aetna flamma; tu, donec cinis
Iniuriosis aridus ventis ferar,
Cales venenis officina Colchicis. 35
Quae finis aut quod me manet stipendium?
Effare; iussas cum fide poenas luam,
Paratus expiare, seu poposceris
Centum iuvencos, sive mendaci lyra
Voles sonari: 'Tu pudica, tu proba 40
Perambulabis astra sidus aureum.'
Infamis Helenae Castor offensus vicem
Fraterque magni Castoris, victi prece,
Adempta vati reddidere lumina:
Et tu—potes nam—solve me dementia, 45
O nec paternis obsoleta sordibus,
Nec in sepulcris pauperum prudens anus
Novendialis dissipare pulveres.
Tibi hospitale pectus et purae manus
Tuusque venter Pactumeius, et tuo 50

Cruore rubros obstetrix pannos lavit,
Utcumque fortis exsilis puerpera.'
'Quid obseratis auribus fundis preces?
Non saxa nudis surdiora navitis
Neptunus alto tundit hibernus salo.
Inultus ut tu riseris Cotyttia
Volgata, sacrum liberi Cupidinis,
Et Esquilini pontifex venefici
Impune ut urbem nomine impleris meo?
Quid proderit ditasse Paelignas anus, 60
Velociusve miscuisse toxicum?
Sed tardiora fata te votis manent;
Ingrata misero vita ducendast in hoc,
Novis ut usque suppetas laboribus.
Optat quietem Pelopis infidi pater, 65
Egens benignae Tantalus semper dapis,
Optat Prometheus obligatus aliti,
Optat supremo collocare Sisyphus
In monte saxum; sed vetant leges Iovis.
Voles modo altis desilire turribus, 70
Modo ense pectus Norico recludere,
Frustraque vincla gutturi nectes tuo,
Fastidiosa tristis aegrimonia.
Vectabor umeris tunc ego inimicis eques,
Meaeque terra cedet insolentiae. 75
An quae movere cereas imagines,
Ut ipse nosti curiosus, et polo
Deripere Lunam vocibus possim meis,
Possim crematos excitare mortuos
Desiderique temperare pocula, 80
Plorem artis in te nil agentis exitus?'

THE ODES AND CARMEN SAECULARE OF HORACE

TRANSLATED INTO ENGLISH VERSE BY JOHN CONINGTON, M.A. CORPUS PROFESSOR OF LATIN IN THE UNIVERSITY OF OXFORD.

PREFACE.

I scarcely know what excuse I can offer for making public this attempt to "translate the untranslatable." No one can be more convinced than I am that a really successful translator must be himself an original poet; and where the author translated happens to be one whose special characteristic is incommunicable grace of expression, the demand on the translator's powers would seem to be indefinitely increased. Yet the time appears to be gone by when men of great original gifts could find satisfaction in reproducing the thoughts and words of others; and the work, if done at all, must now be done by writers of inferior pretension. Among these, however, there are still degrees; and the experience which I have gained since I first adventured as a poetical translator has made me doubt whether I may not be ill-advised in resuming the experiment under any circumstances. Still, an experiment of this kind may have an advantage of its own, even when it is unsuccessful; it may serve as a piece of embodied criticism, showing what the experimenter conceived to be the conditions of success, and may thus, to borrow Horace's own metaphor of the whetstone, impart to others a quality which it is itself without. Perhaps I may be allowed, for a few moments, to combine precept with example, and imitate my distinguished friend and colleague, Professor Arnold, in offering some counsels to the future translator of Horace's Odes, referring, at the same time, by way of illustration, to my own attempt.

The first thing at which, as it seems to me, a Horatian translator ought to aim, is some kind of metrical conformity to his original. Without this we are in danger of losing not only the metrical, but the general effect of the Latin; we express ourselves in a different compass, and the character of the expression is altered accordingly. For instance, one of Horace's leading features is his occasional sententiousness. It is this, perhaps more than anything else, that has made him a storehouse of quotations. He condenses a general truth in a few words, and thus makes his wisdom portable. "Non, si male nunc, et olim sic erit;" "Nihil est ab omni parte beatum;" "Omnes eodem cogimur,"—these and similar expressions remain in the memory when other features of Horace's style, equally characteristic, but less obvious, are forgotten. It is almost impossible for a translator to do justice to this sententious brevity unless the stanza in which he writes is in some sort analogous to the metre of Horace. If he chooses a longer and more diffuse measure, he will be apt to spoil the proverb by expansion; not to mention that much will often depend on the very position of the sentence in the stanza. Perhaps, in order to preserve these external peculiarities, it may be necessary to recast the expression, to substitute, in fact, one form of proverb for another; but this is far preferable to retaining the words in a diluted form, and so losing what gives them their character, I cannot doubt, then, that it is necessary in translating an Ode of Horace to choose some analogous metre; as little can I doubt that a translator of the Odes should appropriate to each Ode some particular metre as its own. It may be true that Horace himself does not invariably suit his metre to his subject; the solemn Alcaic is used for a poem in dispraise of serious thought and praise of wine; the Asclepiad stanza in which Quintilius is lamented is employed to describe the loves of Maecenas and Licymnia. But though this consideration may influence us in our choice of an English metre, it is no reason for not adhering to the one which we may have chosen. If we translate an Alcaic and a Sapphic Ode into the same English measure, because the feeling in both appears to be the same, we are sure to sacrifice some important characteristic of the original in the case of one or the other, perhaps of both. It is better to try to make an English metre more flexible than to use two different English metres to represent two different aspects of one measure in Latin. I am sorry to say that I have myself deviated from this rule occasionally, under circumstances which I shall soon have to explain; but though I may perhaps succeed in showing that my offences have not been serious, I believe the rule itself to be one of universal application, always honoured in the observance, if not always equally dishonoured in the breach.

The question, what metres should be selected, is of course one of very great difficulty. I can only explain what my own practice has been, with some of the reasons which have influenced me in particular cases. Perhaps we may take Milton's celebrated translation of the Ode to Pyrrha as a starting point. There can be no doubt that to an English reader the metre chosen does give much of the effect of the original; yet the resemblance depends rather on the length of the respective lines than on any similarity in the cadences. But it is evident that he chose the iambic movement as the ordinary movement of English poetry; and it is evident, I think, that in translating Horace we shall be right in doing the same, as a general rule. Anapaestic and other rhythms may be beautiful and appropriate in themselves, but they cannot be manipulated so easily; the stanzas with which they are associated bear no resemblance, as stanzas, to the stanzas of Horace's Odes. I have then followed Milton in appropriating the measure in question to the Latin metre, technically called the fourth Asclepiad, at the same time that I have substituted rhyme for blank verse, believing rhyme to be an inferior artist's only chance of giving pleasure. There still remains a question about the distribution of the rhymes, which here, as in most other cases, I have chosen to make alternate. Successive rhymes have their advantages, but they do not give the effect of interlinking, which is so natural in a stanza; the quatrain is reduced to two couplets, and its unity is gone. From the fourth to the third Asclepiad the step is easy. Taking an English iambic line of ten syllables to represent the longer lines of the Latin, an English iambic line of six syllables to represent the shorter, we see that the metre of Horace's "Scriberis Vario" finds its representative in the metre of Mr. Tennyson's "Dream of Fair Women." My experience would lead me to believe the English metre to be quite capable, in really skilful hands, of preserving the effect of the Latin, though, as I have said above, the Latin measure is employed by Horace both for a threnody and for a love-song.

The Sapphic and the Alcaic involve more difficult questions. Here, however, as in the Asclepiad, I believe we must be guided, to some extent, by external similarity. We must choose the iambic movement as being most congenial to English; we must avoid the ten-syllable iambic as already appropriated to the longer Asclepiad line. This leads me to conclude that the staple of each stanza should be the eight-syllable iambic, a measure more familiar to English lyric poetry than any other, and as such well adapted to represent the most familiar lyric measures of Horace. With regard to the Sapphic, it seems desirable that it should be represented by a measure of which the three first lines are eight-syllable iambics, the fourth some shorter variety. Of this stanza there are at least two kinds for which something might be said. It might be constructed so that the three first lines should rhyme with each other, the fourth being otherwise dealt with; or it might be framed on the plan of alternate rhymes, the fourth line still being shorter than the rest. Of the former kind two or three specimens are to be found in Francis' translation of Horace. In these the fourth line consists of but three syllables, the two last of which rhyme with the two last syllables of the fourth line of the next succeeding stanza, as for instance:—

> You shoot; she whets her tusks to bite;
> While he who sits to judge the fight
> Treads on the palm with foot so white,
>   Disdainful,
> And sweetly floating in the air
> Wanton he spreads his fragrant hair,
> Like Ganymede or Nireus fair,
>   And vainful.

It would be possible, no doubt, to produce verses better adapted to recommend the measure than these stanzas, which are, however, the best that can be quoted from Francis; it might be possible, too, to suggest some improvement in the structure of the fourth line. But, however managed, this stanza would, I think, be open to two serious objections; the difficulty of finding three suitable rhymes for each stanza, and the difficulty of disposing of the fourth line, which, if made to rhyme with the fourth line of the next stanza, produces an awkwardness in the case of those Odes which consist of an odd number of stanzas (a large proportion of the whole amount), if left unrhymed, creates an obviously disagreeable effect. We come then to the other alternative, the stanza with alternate rhymes. Here the question is about the fourth line, which may either consist of six syllables, like Coleridge's Fragment, "O leave the lily on its stem," or of four, as in Pope's youthful "Ode on Solitude," these types being further varied by the addition of an extra syllable to form a double rhyme. Of these the four-syllable type seems to me the one to be preferred, as giving the effect of the Adonic better than if it had been two syllables longer. The double rhyme has, I think, an advantage over the single, were it not for its greater difficulty. Much as English lyric poetry owes to double rhymes, a regular supply of them is not easy to procure; some of them are apt to be cumbrous, such as words in-ATION; others, such as the participial-ING (DYING, FLYING, &c.), spoil the language of poetry, leading to the employment of participles where participles are not wanted, and of verbal substantives that exist nowhere else. My first intention was to adopt the double rhyme in this measure, and I accordingly executed three Odes on that plan (Book I. Odes 22, 38; Book II. Ode 16); afterwards I abandoned it, and contented myself with the single rhyme. On the whole, I certainly think this measure answers sufficiently well to the Latin Sapphic; but I have felt its brevity painfully in almost every Ode that I have attempted, being constantly obliged to omit some part of the Latin which I would gladly have preserved. The great number of monosyllables in English is of course a reason for acquiescing in lines shorter than the corresponding lines in Latin; but even in English polysyllables are often necessary, and still oftener desirable on grounds of harmony; and an allowance of twenty-eight syllables of English for thirty-eight of Latin is, after all, rather short.

For the place of the Alcaic there are various candidates. Mr. Tennyson has recently invented a measure which, if not intended to reproduce the Alcaic, was doubtless suggested by it, that which appears in his poem of "The Daisy," and, in a slightly different form, in the "Lines to Mr. Maurice." The two last lines of the latter form of the stanza are indeed evidently copied from the Alcaic, with the simple omission of the last syllable of the last line of the original. Still, as a whole, I doubt whether this form would be as suitable, at least for a dignified Ode, as the other, where the initial iambic in the last line, substituted for a trochee, makes the movement different. I was deterred, however, from attempting either, partly by a doubt whether either had been sufficiently naturalized in English to be safely practised by an unskilful hand, partly by the obvious difficulty of having to provide three rhymes per stanza, against which the occurrence of one line in each without a rhyme at all was but a poor set-off. A second metre which occurred to me is that of Andrew Marvel's Horatian Ode, a variety of which is found twice in Mr. Keble's Christian Year. Here two lines of eight syllables are followed by two of six, the difference between the types being that in Marvel's Ode the rhymes are successive, in Mr. Keble's alternate. The external correspondence between this and the Alcaic is considerable; but the brevity of the English measure struck me at once as a fatal obstacle, and I did not try to encounter it. A third possibility is the stanza of "In Memoriam," which has been adopted by the clever author of "Poems and Translations, by C. S. C.," in his version of "Justum et tenacem." I think it very probable that this will be found eventually to be the best representation of the Alcaic in English, especially as it appears to afford facilities for that linking of stanza to stanza which one who wishes to adhere closely to the logical and rhythmical structure of the Latin soon learns to desire. But I have not adopted it; and I believe there is good reason for not doing so. With all its advantages, it has the patent disadvantage of having been brought into notice by a poet who is influencing the present generation as only a great living poet can. A great writer now, an inferior writer hereafter, may be able to handle it with some degree of independence; but the majority of those who use it at present are sure in adopting Mr. Tennyson's metre to adopt his manner. It is no reproach to "C. S. C." that his Ode reminds us of Mr. Tennyson; it is a praise to him that the recollection is a pleasant one. But Mr. Tennyson's manner is not the manner of Horace, and it is the manner of a contemporary; the expression—a most powerful and beautiful expression—of influences to which a translator of an ancient classic feels himself to be too much subjected already. What is wanted is a metre which shall have other associations than those of the nineteenth century, which shall be the growth of various periods of English poetry, and so be independent of any. Such a metre is that which I have been led to choose, the eight-syllable iambic with alternate rhymes. It is one of the commonest metres in the language, and for that reason it is adapted to more than one class of subjects, to the gay as well as to the grave. But I am mistaken if it is not peculiarly suited to express that concentrated grandeur, that majestic combination of high eloquence with high poetry, which make the early Alcaic Odes of Horace's Third Book what they are to us. The main difficulty is in accommodating its structure to that of the Latin, of varying the pauses, and of linking stanza to stanza. It is a difficulty before which I have felt myself almost powerless, and I have in consequence been driven to the natural expedient of weakness, compromise, sometimes evading it, sometimes coping with it unsuccessfully. In other respects I may be allowed to say that I have found the metre pleasanter to handle than any of the others that I have attempted, except, perhaps, that of "The Dream of Fair Women." The proportion of syllables in each stanza of English to each stanza of Latin is not much greater than in the case of the Sapphic, thirty-two against forty-one; yet, except in a few passages, chiefly those containing proper names, I have had no disagreeable sense of confinement. I believe the reason of this to be that the Latin Alcaic generally contains fewer words in proportion than the Latin Sapphic, the former being favourable to long words, the latter to short ones, as may be seen by contrasting such lines as "Dissentientis conditionibus" with such as "Dona praesentis rape laetus horae ac." This, no doubt, shows that there is an inconvenience in applying the same English iambic measure to two metres which differ so greatly in their practical result; but so far as I can see at present, the evil appears to be one of those which it is wiser to submit to than to attempt to cure.

The problem of finding English representatives for the other Horatian metres, if a more difficult, is a less important one. The most pressing case is that of the metre known as the second Asclepiad, the "Sic te diva potens Cypri." With this, I fear, I shall be thought to have dealt rather capriciously, having rendered it by four different measures, three of them, however, varieties of the same general type. It so happens that the first Ode which I translated was the celebrated Amoebean Poem, the dialogue between Horace and Lydia. I had had at that time not the most distant notion of translating the whole of the Odes, or even any considerable number of them, so that in choosing a metre I thought simply of the requirements of the Ode in question, not of those of the rest of its class. Indeed, I may say that it was the thought of the metre which led me to try if I could translate the Ode. Having accomplished my attempt, I turned to another Ode of the same class, the scarcely less celebrated "Quem tu, Melpomene." For this I took a different metre, which happens to be identical with that of a solitary Ode in the Second Book, "Non ebur neque aureum," being guided still by my feeling about the individual Ode, not by any more general considerations. I did not attempt a third until I had proceeded sufficiently far in my undertaking to see that I should probably continue to the end. Then I had to consider the question of a uniform metre to answer to the Latin. Both of those which I had already tried were rendered impracticable by a double rhyme, which, however manageable in one or two Odes, is unmanageable, as I have before intimated, in the case of a large number. The former of the two measures, divested of the double rhyme, would, I think, lose most of its attractiveness; the latter suffers much less from the privation: the latter accordingly I chose. The trochaic character of the first line seems to me to give it an advantage over any metre composed of pure iambics, if it were only that it discriminates it from those alternate ten-syllable and eight-syllable iambics into which it would be natural to render many of the Epodes. At the same time, it did not appear worth while to rewrite the two Odes already translated, merely for the sake of uniformity, as the principle of correspondence to the Latin, the alternation of longer and shorter lines, is really the same in all three cases. Nay, so tentative has been my treatment of the whole matter, that I have even translated one Ode, the third of Book I, into successive rather than into alternate rhymes, so that readers may judge of the comparative effect of the two varieties. After this confession of irregularity, I need scarcely mention that on coming to the Ode which had suggested the metre in its unmutilated state, I translated it into the mutilated form, not caring either to encounter the inconvenience of the double rhymes, or to make confusion worse confounded by giving it, what it has in the Latin, a separate form of its own.

The remaining metres may be dismissed in a very few words. As a general rule, I have avoided couplets of any sort, and chosen some kind of stanza. As a German critic has pointed out, all the Odes of Horace, with one doubtful exception, may be reduced to quatrains; and though this peculiarity does not, so far as we can see, affect the character of any of the Horatian metres (except, of course, those that are written in stanzas), or influence the structure of the Latin, it must be considered as a happy circumstance for those who wish to render Horace into English. In respect of restraint, indeed, the English couplet may sometimes be less inconvenient than the quatrain, as it is, on the whole, easier to run couplet into couplet than to run quatrain into quatrain; but the couplet seems hardly suitable for an English lyrical poem of any length, the very notion of lyrical poetry apparently involving a complexity which can only be represented by rhymes recurring at intervals. In the case of one of the three poems written by Horace in the measure called the greater Asclepiad, ("Tu ne quoesieris,") I have adopted the couplet; in another ("Nullam, Vare,") the quatrain, the determining reason in the two cases being the length of the two Odes, the former of which consists but of eight lines, the latter of sixteen. The metre which I selected for each is the thirteen- syllable trochaic of "Locksley Hall;" and it is curious to observe the different effect of the metre according as it is written in two lines or in four. In the "Locksley Hall" couplet its movement is undoubtedly trochaic; but when it is expanded into a quatrain, as in Mrs. Browning's poem of "Lady Geraldine's Courtship," the movement changes, and instead of a more or less equal stress on the alternate syllables, the full ictus is only felt in one syllable out of every four; in ancient metrical language the metre becomes Ionic a minore. This very Ionic a minore is itself, I need not say, the metre of a single Ode in the Third Book, the "Miserarum est," and I have devised a stanza for it, taking much more pains with the apportionment of the ictus than in the case of the trochaic quatrain, which is better able to modulate itself. I have also ventured to invent a metre for that technically known as the Fourth Archilochian, the "Solvitur acris hiems," by combining the fourteen-syllable with the ten-syllable iambic in an alternately rhyming stanza. [Footnote: I may be permitted to mention that Lord Derby, in a volume of Translations printed privately before the appearance of this work, has employed the same measure in rendering the same Ode, the only difference being that his rhymes are not alternate, but successive.] The First Archilochian, "Diffugere nives," I have represented by a combination of the ten-syllable with the four- syllable iambic. For the so-called greater Sapphic, the "Lydia, die per omnes" I have made another iambic combination, the six-syllable with the fourteen-syllable, arranged as a couplet. The choriambic I thought might be exchanged for a heroic stanza, in which the first line should rhyme with the fourth, the second with the third, a kind of "In Memoriam" elongated. Lastly, I have chosen the heroic quatrain proper, the metre of Gray's "Elegy," for the two Odes in the First Book written in what is called the Metrum Alcmanium, "Laudabunt alii," and "Te maris et terrae," rather from a vague notion of the dignity of the measure than from any distinct sense of special appropriateness.

From this enumeration, which I fear has been somewhat tedious, it will be seen that I have been guided throughout not by any systematic principles, but by a multitude of minor considerations, some operating more strongly in one case, and some in another. I trust, however, that in all this diversity I shall be found to have kept in view the object on which I have been insisting, a metrical correspondence with the original. Even where I have been most inconsistent, I have still adhered to the rule of comprising the English within the same number of lines as the Latin. I believe tills to be almost essential to the preservation of the character of the Horatian lyric, which always retains a certain severity, and never loses itself in modern exuberance; and though I am well aware that the result in my case has frequently, perhaps generally, been a most un-Horatian stiffness, I am convinced from my own experience that a really accomplished artist would find the task of composing under these conditions far more hopeful than he had previously imagined it to be. Yet it is a restraint to which scarcely any of the previous translators of the Odes have been willing to submit. Perhaps Professor Newman is the only one who has carried it through the whole of the Four Books; most of my predecessors have ignored it altogether. It is this which, in my judgment, is the chief drawback to the success of the most distinguished of them, Mr. Theodore Martin. He has brought to his work a grace and delicacy of expression and a happy flow of musical verse which are beyond my praise, and which render many of his Odes most pleasing to read as poems. I wish he had combined with these qualities that terseness and condensation which remind us that a Roman, even when writing "songs of love and wine," was a Roman still.

Some may consider it extraordinary that in discussing the different ways of representing Horatian metres I have said nothing of transplanting those metres themselves into English. I think, however, that an apology for my silence may he found in the present state of the controversy about the English hexameter. Whatever may be the ultimate fate of that struggling alien—and I confess myself to be one of those who doubt whether he can ever be naturalized—most judges will, I believe, agree that for the present at any rate his case is sufficient to occupy the literary tribunals, and that to raise any discussion on the rights of others of his class would be premature. Practice, after all, is more powerful in such matters than theory; and hardly at any time in the three hundred years during which we have had a formed literature has the introduction of classical lyric measures into English been a practical question. Stanihurst has had many successors in the hexameter; probably he has not had more than one or two in the Asclepiad. The Sapphic, indeed, has been tried repeatedly; but it is an exception which is no exception, the metre thus intruded into our language not being really the Latin Sapphic, but a metre of a different kind, founded on a mistake in the manner of reading the Latin, into which Englishmen naturally fall, and in which, for convenience' sake, they as naturally persist. The late Mr. Clough, whose efforts in literature were essentially tentative, in form as well as in spirit, and whose loss for that very reason is perhaps of more serious import to English poetry than if, with equal genius, he had possessed a more conservative habit of mind, once attempted reproductions of nearly all the different varieties of Horatian metres. They may he found in a paper which he contributed to the fourth volume of the "Classical Museum;" and a perusal of them will, I think, be likely to convince the reader that the task is one in which even great rhythmical power and mastery of language would be far from certain of succeeding. Even the Alcaic fragment which he has inserted in his "Amours de Voyage"—

"Eager for battle here
Stood Vulcan, here matronal Juno,

And with the bow to his shoulder faithful
He who with pure dew laveth of Castaly
His flowing locks, who holdeth of Lycia
The oak forest and the wood that bore him,
Delos' and Patara's own Apollo,"—

admirably finished as it is, and highly pleasing as a fragment, scarcely persuades us
that twenty stanzas of the same workmanship would be read with adequate pleasure,
still less that the same satisfaction would be felt through six-and-thirty Odes. After all,
however, a sober critic will be disposed rather to pass judgment on the past than to
predict the future, knowing, as he must, how easily the "solvitur ambulando" of an
artist like Mr. Tennyson may disturb a whole chain of ingenious reasoning on the
possibilities of things.

The question of the language into which Horace should be translated is not less
important than that of the metre; but it involves far less discussion of points of detail,
and may, in fact, be very soon dismissed. I believe that the chief danger which a
translator has to avoid is that of subjection to the influences of his own period.
Whether or no Mr. Merivale is right in supposing that an analogy exists between the
literature of the present day and that of post-Augustan Rome, it will not, I think, be
disputed that between our period and the Augustan period the resemblances are very
few, perhaps not more than must necessarily exist between two periods of high
cultivation. It is the fashion to say that the characteristic of the literature of the last
century was shallow clearness, the expression of obvious thoughts in obvious, though
highly finished language; it is the fashion to retort upon our own generation that its
tendency is to over-thinking and over-expression, a constant search for thoughts
which shall not be obvious and words which shall be above the level of received
conventionality. Accepting these as descriptions, however imperfect, of two different
types of literature, we can have no doubt to which division to refer the literary
remains of Augustan Rome. The Odes of Horace, in particular, will, I think, strike a
reader who comes back to them after reading other books, as distinguished by a
simplicity, monotony, and almost poverty of sentiment, and as depending for the
charm of their external form not so much on novel and ingenious images as on
musical words aptly chosen and aptly combined. We are always hearing of wine-jars
and Thracian convivialities, of parsley wreaths and Syrian nard; the graver topics,
which it is the poet's wisdom to forget, are constantly typified by the terrors of
quivered Medes and painted Gelonians; there is the perpetual antithesis between
youth and age, there is the ever-recurring image of green and withered trees, and it is
only the attractiveness of the Latin, half real, half perhaps arising from association
and the romance of a language not one's own, that makes us feel this "lyrical
commonplace" more supportable than common-place is usually found to be. It is this,
indeed, which constitutes the grand difficulty of the translator, who may well despair
when he undertakes to reproduce beauties depending on expression by a process in
which expression is sure to be sacrificed. But it would, I think, be a mistake to attempt
to get rid of this monotony by calling in the aid of that variety of images and forms of
language which modern poetry presents. Here, as in the case of metres, it seems to me
that to exceed the bounds of what may be called classical parsimony would be to
abandon the one chance, faint as it may be, of producing on the reader's mind
something like the impression produced by Horace. I do not say that I have always
been as abstinent as I think a translator ought to be; here, as in all matters connected

with this most difficult work, weakness may claim a licence of which strength would disdain to avail itself; I only say that I have not surrendered myself to the temptation habitually and without a struggle. As a general rule, while not unfrequently compelled to vary the precise image Horace has chosen, I have substituted one which he has used elsewhere; where he has talked of triumphs, meaning no more than victories, I have talked of bays; where he gives the picture of the luxuriant harvests of Sardinia, I have spoken of the wheat on the threshing-floors. On the whole I have tried, so far as my powers would allow me, to give my translation something of the colour of our eighteenth-century poetry, believing the poetry of that time to be the nearest analogue of the poetry of Augustus' court that England has produced, and feeling quite sure that a writer will bear traces enough of the language and manner of his own time to redeem him from the charge of having forgotten what is after all his native tongue. As one instance out of many, I may mention the use of compound epithets as a temptation to which the translator of Horace is sure to be exposed, and which, in my judgment, he ought in general to resist. Their power of condensation naturally recommends them to a writer who has to deal with inconvenient clauses, threatening to swallow up the greater part of a line; but there is no doubt that in the Augustan poets, as compared with the poets of the republic, they are chiefly conspicuous for their absence, and it is equally certain, I think, that a translator of an Augustan poet ought not to suffer them to be a prominent feature of his style. I have, perhaps, indulged in them too often myself to note them as a defect in others; but it seems to me that they contribute, along with the Tennysonian metre, to diminish the pleasure with which we read such a version as that of which I have already spoken by "C. S. C." of "Justum et tenacem." I may add, too, that I have occasionally allowed the desire of brevity to lead me into an omission of the definite article, which, though perhaps in keeping with the style of Milton, is certainly out of keeping with that of the eighteenth century. It is one of a translator's many refuges, and has been conceded so long that it can hardly he denied him with justice, however it may remind the reader of a bald verbal rendering.

A very few words will serve to conclude this somewhat protracted Preface. I have not sought to interpret Horace with the minute accuracy which I should think necessary in writing a commentary; and in general I have been satisfied to consult two of the latest editions, those by Orelli and Ritter. In a few instances I have preferred the views of the latter; but his edition will not supersede that of the former, whose commentary is one of the most judicious ever produced, within a moderate compass, upon a classical author. In the few notes which I have added at the end of this volume, I have noticed chiefly the instances in which I have differed from him, in favour either of Hitter's interpretation, or of some view of my own. At the same time it must be said that my translation is not to be understood as always indicating the interpretation I prefer. Sometimes, where the general effect of two views of the construction of a passage has been the same, I have followed that which I believed to be less correct, for reasons of convenience. I have of course held myself free to deviate in a thousand instances from the exact form of the Latin sentence; and it did not seem reasonable to debar myself from a mode of expression which appeared generally consistent with the original, because it happened to be verbally consistent with a mistaken view of the Latin words. To take an example mentioned in my notes, it may be better in Book III. Ode 3, line 25, to make "adulterae" the genitive case after "hospes" than the dative after "splendet;" but for practical purposes the two come to the same thing, both being included in the full development of the thought; and a translation which represents either is substantially a true translation. I have omitted four Odes altogether, one in each Book, and some stanzas of a fifth; and in some other instances I have been studiously paraphrastic. Nor have I thought it worth while to extend my translation from the Odes to the Epodes. The Epodes were the production of Horace's youth, and probably would not have been much cared for by posterity if they had constituted his only title to fame. A few of them are beautiful, but some are revolting, and the rest, as pictures of a roving and sensual passion, remind us of the least attractive portion of the Odes. In the case of a writer like Horace it is not easy to draw an exact line; but though in the Odes our admiration of much that is graceful and tender and even true may balance our moral repugnance to many parts of the poet's philosophy of life, it does not seem equally desirable to dwell minutely on a class of compositions where the beauties are fewer and the deformities more numerous and more undisguised.

I should add that any coincidences that may be noticed between my version and those of my predecessors are, for the most part, merely coincidences. In some cases I may have knowingly borrowed a rhyme, but only where the rhyme was too common to have created a right of property.

PREFACE TO SECOND EDITION.

I am very sensible of the favour which has carried this translation from a first edition into a second. The interval between the two has been too short to admit of my altering my judgment in any large number of instances; but I have been glad to employ the present opportunity in amending, as I hope, an occasional word or expression, and, in one or two cases, recasting a stanza. The notices which my book has received, and the opinions communicated by the kindness of friends, have been gratifying to me, both in themselves, and as showing the interest which is being felt in the subject of Horatian translation. It is not surprising that there should be considerable differences of opinion about the manner in which Horace is to be rendered, and also about the metre appropriate to particular Odes; but I need not say that it is through such discussion that questions like these advance towards settlement. It would indeed be a satisfaction to me to think that the question of translating Horace had been brought a step nearer to its solution by the experiment which I again venture to submit to the public.

PREFACE TO THIRD EDITION.

The changes which I have made in this impression of my translation are somewhat more numerous than those which I was able to introduce into the last, as might be expected from the longer interval between the times of publication; but the work may still be spoken of as substantially unaltered.

THE ODES OF HORACE.

BOOK I.

I.

MAECENAS ATAVIS.

Maecenas, born of monarch ancestors,
  The shield at once and glory of my life!
  There are who joy them in the Olympic strife
And love the dust they gather in the course;
The goal by hot wheels shunn'd, the famous prize,
  Exalt them to the gods that rule mankind;
  This joys, if rabbles fickle as the wind
Through triple grade of honours bid him rise,
That, if his granary has stored away
  Of Libya's thousand floors the yield entire;
  The man who digs his field as did his sire,
With honest pride, no Attalus may sway
By proffer'd wealth to tempt Myrtoan seas,
  The timorous captain of a Cyprian bark.
  The winds that make Icarian billows dark
The merchant fears, and hugs the rural ease
Of his own village home; but soon, ashamed
  Of penury, he refits his batter'd craft.
  There is, who thinks no scorn of Massic draught,
Who robs the daylight of an hour unblamed,
Now stretch'd beneath the arbute on the sward,
  Now by some gentle river's sacred spring;
  Some love the camp, the clarion's joyous ring,
And battle, by the mother's soul abhorr'd.
See, patient waiting in the clear keen air,
  The hunter, thoughtless of his delicate bride,
  Whether the trusty hounds a stag have eyed,
Or the fierce Marsian boar has burst the snare.
To me the artist's meed, the ivy wreath
  Is very heaven: me the sweet cool of woods,
  Where Satyrs frolic with the Nymphs, secludes
From rabble rout, so but Euterpe's breath
Fail not the flute, nor Polyhymnia fly
  Averse from stringing new the Lesbian lyre.
  O, write my name among that minstrel choir,
And my proud head shall strike upon the sky!

II.

JAM SATIS TERRIS.

Enough of snow and hail at last
  The Sire has sent in vengeance down:
His bolts, at His own temple cast,
    Appall'd the town,
Appall'd the lands, lest Pyrrha's time
  Return, with all its monstrous sights,
When Proteus led his flocks to climb
    The flatten'd heights,
When fish were in the elm-tops caught,
  Where once the stock-dove wont to bide,
And does were floating, all distraught,
    Adown the tide.
Old Tiber, hurl'd in tumult back
  From mingling with the Etruscan main,
Has threaten'd Numa's court with wrack
    And Vesta's fane.
Roused by his Ilia's plaintive woes,
  He vows revenge for guiltless blood,
And, spite of Jove, his banks o'erflows,
    Uxorious flood.
Yes, Fame shall tell of civic steel
  That better Persian lives had spilt,
To youths, whose minish'd numbers feel
    Their parents' guilt.
What god shall Rome invoke to stay
  Her fall? Can suppliance overbear
The ear of Vesta, turn'd away
    From chant and prayer?
Who comes, commission'd to atone
  For crime like ours? at length appear,
A cloud round thy bright shoulders thrown,
    Apollo seer!
Or Venus, laughter-loving dame,
  Round whom gay Loves and Pleasures fly;
Or thou, if slighted sons may claim
    A parent's eye,
O weary—with thy long, long game,
  Who lov'st fierce shouts and helmets bright,
And Moorish warrior's glance of flame
    Or e'er he smite!
Or Maia's son, if now awhile
  In youthful guise we see thee here,
Caesar's avenger—such the style
    Thou deign'st to bear;
Late be thy journey home, and long

Thy sojourn with Rome's family;
Nor let thy wrath at our great wrong
    Lend wings to fly.
Here take our homage, Chief and Sire;
  Here wreathe with bay thy conquering brow,
And bid the prancing Mede retire,
    Our Caesar thou!

III.

SIC TE DIVA.

Thus may Cyprus' heavenly queen,
Thus Helen's brethren, stars of brightest sheen,
  Guide thee! May the Sire of wind
Each truant gale, save only Zephyr, bind!
  So do thou, fair ship, that ow'st
Virgil, thy precious freight, to Attic coast,
  Safe restore thy loan and whole,
And save from death the partner of my soul!
  Oak and brass of triple fold
Encompass'd sure that heart, which first made bold
  To the raging sea to trust
A fragile bark, nor fear'd the Afric gust
  With its Northern mates at strife,
Nor Hyads' frown, nor South-wind fury-rife,
  Mightiest power that Hadria knows,
Wills he the waves to madden or compose.
  What had Death in store to awe
Those eyes, that huge sea-beasts unmelting saw,
  Saw the swelling of the surge,
And high Ceraunian cliffs, the seaman's scourge?
  Heaven's high providence in vain
Has sever'd countries with the estranging main,
  If our vessels ne'ertheless
With reckless plunge that sacred bar transgress.
  Daring all, their goal to win,
Men tread forbidden ground, and rush on sin:
  Daring all, Prometheus play'd
His wily game, and fire to man convey'd;
  Soon as fire was stolen away,
Pale Fever's stranger host and wan Decay
  Swept o'er earth's polluted face,
And slow Fate quicken'd Death's once halting pace.
  Daedalus the void air tried
On wings, to humankind by Heaven denied;
  Acheron's bar gave way with ease

Before the arm of labouring Hercules.
　Nought is there for man too high;
Our impious folly e'en would climb the sky,
　Braves the dweller on the steep,
Nor lets the bolts of heavenly vengeance sleep.

IV.

SOLVITUR ACRIS HIEMS.

The touch of Zephyr and of Spring has loosen'd Winter's thrall;
　The well-dried keels are wheel'd again to sea:
The ploughman cares not for his fire, nor cattle for their stall,
　And frost no more is whitening all the lea.
Now Cytherea leads the dance, the bright moon overhead;
　The Graces and the Nymphs, together knit,
With rhythmic feet the meadow beat, while Vulcan, fiery red,
　Heats the Cyclopian forge in Aetna's pit.
'Tis now the time to wreathe the brow with branch of myrtle green,
　Or flowers, just opening to the vernal breeze;
Now Faunus claims his sacrifice among the shady treen,
　Lambkin or kidling, which soe'er he please.
Pale Death, impartial, walks his round; he knocks at cottage-gate
　And palace-portal. Sestius, child of bliss!
How should a mortal's hopes be long, when short his being's date?
　Lo here! the fabulous ghosts, the dark abyss,
The void of the Plutonian hall, where soon as e'er you go,
　No more for you shall leap the auspicious die
To seat you on the throne of wine; no more your breast shall glow
　For Lycidas, the star of every eye.

V.

QUIS MULTA GRACILIS.

What slender youth, besprinkled with perfume,
　Courts you on roses in some grotto's shade?
　Fair Pyrrha, say, for whom
　　Your yellow hair you braid,
So trim, so simple! Ah! how oft shall he
　Lament that faith can fail, that gods can change,
　　Viewing the rough black sea
　　　With eyes to tempests strange,

Who now is basking in your golden smile,
  And dreams of you still fancy-free, still kind,
    Poor fool, nor knows the guile
      Of the deceitful wind!
Woe to the eyes you dazzle without cloud
  Untried! For me, they show in yonder fane
    My dripping garments, vow'd
      To Him who curbs the main.

VI.

SCRIBERIS VARIO.

Not I, but Varius:—he, of Homer's brood
  A tuneful swan, shall bear you on his wing,
Your tale of trophies, won by field or flood,
    Mighty alike to sing.
Not mine such themes, Agrippa; no, nor mine
  To chant the wrath that fill'd Pelides' breast,
Nor dark Ulysses' wanderings o'er the brine,
    Nor Pelops' house unblest.
Vast were the task, I feeble; inborn shame,
  And she, who makes the peaceful lyre submit,
Forbid me to impair great Caesar's fame
    And yours by my weak wit.
But who may fitly sing of Mars array'd
  In adamant mail, or Merion, black with dust
Of Troy, or Tydeus' son by Pallas' aid
    Strong against gods to thrust?
Feasts are my theme, my warriors maidens fair,
  Who with pared nails encounter youths in fight;
Be Fancy free or caught in Cupid's snare,
    Her temper still is light.

VII.

LAUDABUNT ALII.

Let others Rhodes or Mytilene sing,
    Or Ephesus, or Corinth, set between
Two seas, or Thebes, or Delphi, for its king
    Each famous, or Thessalian Tempe green;
There are who make chaste Pallas' virgin tower

The daily burden of unending song,
    And search for wreaths the olive's rifled bower;
        The praise of Juno sounds from many a tongue,
Telling of Argos' steeds, Mycenaes's gold.
        For me stern Sparta forges no such spell,
No, nor Larissa's plain of richest mould,
        As bright Albunea echoing from her cell.
O headlong Anio! O Tiburnian groves,
        And orchards saturate with shifting streams!
Look how the clear fresh south from heaven removes
        The tempest, nor with rain perpetual teems!
You too be wise, my Plancus: life's worst cloud
        Will melt in air, by mellow wine allay'd,
Dwell you in camps, with glittering banners proud,
        Or 'neath your Tibur's canopy of shade.
When Teucer fled before his father's frown
        From Salamis, they say his temples deep
He dipp'd in wine, then wreath'd with poplar crown,
        And bade his comrades lay their grief to sleep:
"Where Fortune bears us, than my sire more kind,
        There let us go, my own, my gallant crew.
'Tis Teucer leads, 'tis Teucer breathes the wind;
        No more despair; Apollo's word is true.
Another Salamis in kindlier air
        Shall yet arise. Hearts, that have borne with me
Worse buffets! drown to-day in wine your care;
        To-morrow we recross the wide, wide sea!"

VIII.

LYDIA, DIC PER OMNES.

    Lydia, by all above,
Why bear so hard on Sybaris, to ruin him with love?
    What change has made him shun
The playing-ground, who once so well could bear the dust and sun?
    Why does he never sit
On horseback in his company, nor with uneven bit
    His Gallic courser tame?
Why dreads he yellow Tiber, as 'twould sully that fair frame?
    Like poison loathes the oil,
His arms no longer black and blue with honourable toil,
    He who erewhile was known
For quoit or javelin oft and oft beyond the limit thrown?
    Why skulks he, as they say
Did Thetis' son before the dawn of Ilion's fatal day,

For fear the manly dress
Should fling him into danger's arms, amid the Lycian press?

IX.

VIDES UT ALTA.

See, how it stands, one pile of snow,
  Soracte! 'neath the pressure yield
Its groaning woods; the torrents' flow
  With clear sharp ice is all congeal'd.
Heap high the logs, and melt the cold,
  Good Thaliarch; draw the wine we ask,
That mellower vintage, four-year-old,
  From out the cellar'd Sabine cask.
The future trust with Jove; when He
  Has still'd the warring tempests' roar
On the vex'd deep, the cypress-tree
  And aged ash are rock'd no more.
O, ask not what the morn will bring,
  But count as gain each day that chance
May give you; sport in life's young spring,
  Nor scorn sweet love, nor merry dance,
While years are green, while sullen eld
  Is distant. Now the walk, the game,
The whisper'd talk at sunset held,
  Each in its hour, prefer their claim.
Sweet too the laugh, whose feign'd alarm
  The hiding-place of beauty tells,
The token, ravish'd from the arm
  Or finger, that but ill rebels.

X.

MERCURI FACUNDE.

Grandson of Atlas, wise of tongue,
    O Mercury, whose wit could tame
Man's savage youth by power of song
    And plastic game!
Thee sing I, herald of the sky,
  Who gav'st the lyre its music sweet,
Hiding whate'er might please thine eye

In frolic cheat.
See, threatening thee, poor guileless child,
  Apollo claims, in angry tone,
His cattle;—all at once he smiled,
    His quiver gone.
Strong in thy guidance, Hector's sire
  Escaped the Atridae, pass'd between
Thessalian tents and warders' fire,
    Of all unseen.
Thou lay'st unspotted souls to rest;
  Thy golden rod pale spectres know;
Blest power! by all thy brethren blest,
    Above, below!

XI

TU NE QUAESIERIS.

Ask not ('tis forbidden knowledge), what our destined term of years,
Mine and yours; nor scan the tables of your Babylonish seers.
Better far to bear the future, my Leuconoe, like the past,
Whether Jove has many winters yet to give, or this our last;
THIS, that makes the Tyrrhene billows spend their strength against
    the shore.
Strain your wine and prove your wisdom; life is short; should hope
    be more?
In the moment of our talking, envious time has ebb'd away.
Seize the present; trust to-morrow e'en as little as you may.

XII.

QUEMN VIRUM AUT HEROA.

What man, what hero, Clio sweet,
  On harp or flute wilt thou proclaim?
What god shall echo's voice repeat
  In mocking game
To Helicon's sequester'd shade,
  Or Pindus, or on Haemus chill,
Where once the hurrying woods obey'd
  The minstrel's will,
Who, by his mother's gift of song,
  Held the fleet stream, the rapid breeze,
And led with blandishment along

119

The listening trees?
Whom praise we first? the Sire on high,
  Who gods and men unerring guides,
Who rules the sea, the earth, the sky,
  Their times and tides.
No mightier birth may He beget;
  No like, no second has He known;
Yet nearest to her sire's is set
  Minerva's throne.
Nor yet shall Bacchus pass unsaid,
  Bold warrior, nor the virgin foe
Of savage beasts, nor Phoebus, dread
  With deadly bow.
Alcides too shall be my theme,
  And Leda's twins, for horses be,
He famed for boxing; soon as gleam
  Their stars at sea,
The lash'd spray trickles from the steep,
  The wind sinks down, the storm-cloud flies,
The threatening billow on the deep
  Obedient lies.
Shall now Quirinus take his turn,
  Or quiet Numa, or the state
Proud Tarquin held, or Cato stern,
  By death made great?
Ay, Regulus and the Scaurian name,
  And Paullus, who at Cannae gave
His glorious soul, fair record claim,
  For all were brave.
Thee, Furius, and Fabricius, thee,
  Rough Curius too, with untrimm'd beard,
Your sires' transmitted poverty
  To conquest rear'd.
Marcellus' fame, its up-growth hid,
  Springs like a tree; great Julius' light
Shines, like the radiant moon amid
  The lamps of night.
Dread Sire and Guardian of man's race,
  To Thee, O Jove, the Fates assign
Our Caesar's charge; his power and place
  Be next to Thine.
Whether the Parthian, threatening Rome,
  His eagles scatter to the wind,
Or follow to their eastern home
  Cathay and Ind,
Thy second let him rule below:
  Thy car shall shake the realms above;
Thy vengeful bolts shall overthrow
  Each guilty grove.

XIII.

CUM TU, LYDIA.

Telephus—you praise him still,
    His waxen arms, his rosy-tinted neck;
  Ah! and all the while I thrill
With jealous pangs I cannot, cannot check.
    See, my colour comes and goes,
My poor heart flutters, Lydia, and the dew,
    Down my cheek soft stealing, shows
What lingering torments rack me through and through.
    Oh, 'tis agony to see
Those snowwhite shoulders scarr'd in drunken fray,
    Or those ruby lips, where he
Has left strange marks, that show how rough his play!
    Never, never look to find
A faithful heart in him whose rage can harm
    Sweetest lips, which Venus kind
Has tinctured with her quintessential charm.
    Happy, happy, happy they
Whose living love, untroubled by all strife,
    Binds them till the last sad day,
Nor parts asunder but with parting life!

XIV

O NAVIS, REFERENT.

O LUCKLESS bark! new waves will force you back
To sea. O, haste to make the haven yours!
    E'en now, a helpless wrack,
        You drift, despoil'd of oars;
The Afric gale has dealt your mast a wound;
  Your sailyards groan, nor can your keel sustain,
    Till lash'd with cables round,
        A more imperious main.
Your canvass hangs in ribbons, rent and torn;
  No gods are left to pray to in fresh need.
    A pine of Pontus born
        Of noble forest breed,
You boast your name and lineage—madly blind!
  Can painted timbers quell a seaman's fear?
    Beware! or else the wind
        Makes you its mock and jeer.

Your trouble late made sick this heart of mine,
  And still I love you, still am ill at ease.
    O, shun the sea, where shine
      The thick-sown Cyclades!

XV.

PASTOR CUM TRAHERET.

When the false swain was hurrying o'er the deep
  His Spartan hostess in the Idaean bark,
Old Nereus laid the unwilling winds asleep,
    That all to Fate might hark,
Speaking through him:—"Home in ill hour you take
  A prize whom Greece shall claim with troops untold,
Leagued by an oath your marriage tie to break
    And Priam's kingdom old.
Alas! what deaths you launch on Dardan realm!
  What toils are waiting, man and horse to tire!
See! Pallas trims her aegis and her helm,
    Her chariot and her ire.
Vainly shall you, in Venus' favour strong,
  Your tresses comb, and for your dames divide
On peaceful lyre the several parts of song;
    Vainly in chamber hide
From spears and Gnossian arrows, barb'd with fate,
  And battle's din, and Ajax in the chase
Unconquer'd; those adulterous locks, though late,
    Shall gory dust deface.
Hark! 'tis the death-cry of your race! look back!
  Ulysses comes, and Pylian Nestor grey;
See! Salaminian Teucer on your track,
    And Sthenelus, in the fray
Versed, or with whip and rein, should need require,
  No laggard. Merion too your eyes shall know
From far. Tydides, fiercer than his sire,
    Pursues you, all aglow;
Him, as the stag forgets to graze for fright,
  Seeing the wolf at distance in the glade,
And flies, high panting, you shall fly, despite
    Boasts to your leman made.
What though Achilles' wrathful fleet postpone
  The day of doom to Troy and Troy's proud dames,
Her towers shall fall, the number'd winters flown,
    Wrapp'd in Achaean flames."

XVI.

O MATRE PULCHRA.

O lovelier than the lovely dame
  That bore you, sentence as you please
Those scurril verses, be it flame
  Your vengeance craves, or Hadrian seas.
Not Cybele, nor he that haunts
  Rich Pytho, worse the brain confounds,
Not Bacchus, nor the Corybants
  Clash their loud gongs with fiercer sounds
Than savage wrath; nor sword nor spear
  Appals it, no, nor ocean's frown,
Nor ravening fire, nor Jupiter
  In hideous ruin crashing down.
Prometheus, forced, they say, to add
  To his prime clay some favourite part
From every kind, took lion mad,
  And lodged its gall in man's poor heart.
'Twas wrath that laid Thyestes low;
  'Tis wrath that oft destruction calls
On cities, and invites the foe
  To drive his plough o'er ruin'd walls.
Then calm your spirit; I can tell
  How once, when youth in all my veins
Was glowing, blind with rage, I fell
  On friend and foe in ribald strains.
Come, let me change my sour for sweet,
  And smile complacent as before:
Hear me my palinode repeat,
  And give me back your heart once more.

XVII. VELOX AMOENUM.

The pleasures of Lucretilis
  Tempt Faunus from his Grecian seat;
He keeps my little goats in bliss
  Apart from wind, and rain, and heat.
In safety rambling o'er the sward
  For arbutes and for thyme they peer,
The ladies of the unfragrant lord,
  Nor vipers, green with venom, fear,
Nor savage wolves, of Mars' own breed,
  My Tyndaris, while Ustica's dell
Is vocal with the silvan reed,
  And music thrills the limestone fell.
Heaven is my guardian; Heaven approves

A blameless life, by song made sweet;
Come hither, and the fields and groves
　Their horn shall empty at your feet.
Here, shelter'd by a friendly tree,
　In Teian measures you shall sing
Bright Circe and Penelope,
　Love-smitten both by one sharp sting.
Here shall you quaff beneath the shade
　Sweet Lesbian draughts that injure none,
Nor fear lest Mars the realm invade
　Of Semele's Thyonian son,
Lest Cyrus on a foe too weak
　Lay the rude hand of wild excess,
His passion on your chaplet wreak,
　Or spoil your undeserving dress.

XVIII.

NULLAM, VARE.

Varus, are your trees in planting? put in none before the vine,
　In the rich domain of Tibur, by the walls of Catilus;
There's a power above that hampers all that sober brains design,
　And the troubles man is heir to thus are quell'd, and only thus.
Who can talk of want or warfare when the wine is in his head,
　Not of thee, good father Bacchus, and of Venus fair and bright?
But should any dream of licence, there's a lesson may be read,
　How 'twas wine that drove the Centaurs with the Lapithae to fight.
And the Thracians too may warn us; truth and falsehood, good and
　　ill,
　How they mix them, when the wine-god's hand is heavy on them laid!
Never, never, gracious Bacchus, may I move thee 'gainst thy will,
　Or uncover what is hidden in the verdure of thy shade!
Silence thou thy savage cymbals, and the Berecyntine horn;
　　In their train Self-love still follows, dully, desperately
　　　blind,
And Vain-glory, towering upwards in its empty-headed scorn,
　And the Faith that keeps no secrets, with a window in its mind.

XIX.

MATER SAEVA CUPIDINUM

Cupid's mother, cruel dame,
And Semele's Theban boy, and Licence bold,
    Bid me kindle into flame
This heart, by waning passion now left cold.
    O, the charms of Glycera,
That hue, more dazzling than the Parian stone!
    O, that sweet tormenting play,
That too fair face, that blinds when look'd upon!
    Venus comes in all her might,
Quits Cyprus for my heart, nor lets me tell
    Of the Parthian, hold in flight,
Nor Scythian hordes, nor aught that breaks her spell.
    Heap the grassy altar up,
Bring vervain, boys, and sacred frankincense;
    Fill the sacrificial cup;
A victim's blood will soothe her vehemence.

XX.

VILE POTABIS.

Not large my cups, nor rich my cheer,
    This Sabine wine, which erst I seal'd,
That day the applauding theatre
    Your welcome peal'd,
Dear knight Maecenas! as 'twere fain
    That your paternal river's banks,
And Vatican, in sportive strain,
    Should echo thanks.
For you Calenian grapes are press'd,
    And Caecuban; these cups of mine
Falernum's bounty ne'er has bless'd,
    Nor Formian vine.

XXI.

DIANAM TENERAE.

Of Dian's praises, tender maidens, tell;
    Of Cynthus' unshorn god, young striplings, sing;
        And bright Latona, well
            Beloved of Heaven's high King.
Sing her that streams and silvan foliage loves,
    Whate'er on Algidus' chill brow is seen,

In Erymanthian groves
  Dark-leaved, or Cragus green.
Sing Tempe too, glad youths, in strain as loud,
  And Phoebus' birthplace, and that shoulder fair,
    His golden quiver proud
      And brother's lyre to bear.
His arm shall banish Hunger, Plague, and War
  To Persia and to Britain's coast, away
    From Rome and Caesar far,
      If you have zeal to pray.

XXII.

INTEGER VITAE.

No need of Moorish archer's craft
  To guard the pure and stainless liver;
He wants not, Fuscus, poison'd shaft
    To store his quiver,
Whether he traverse Libyan shoals,
  Or Caucasus, forlorn and horrent,
Or lands where far Hydaspes rolls
    His fabled torrent.
A wolf, while roaming trouble-free
  In Sabine wood, as fancy led me,
Unarm'd I sang my Lalage,
    Beheld, and fled me.
Dire monster! in her broad oak woods
  Fierce Daunia fosters none such other,
Nor Juba's land, of lion broods
    The thirsty mother.
Place me where on the ice-bound plain
  No tree is cheer'd by summer breezes,
Where Jove descends in sleety rain
    Or sullen freezes;
Place me where none can live for heat,
  'Neath Phoebus' very chariot plant me,
That smile so sweet, that voice so sweet,
    Shall still enchant me.

XXIII.

VITAS HINNULEO.

You fly me, Chloe, as o'er trackless hills
  A young fawn runs her timorous dam to find,
    Whom empty terror thrills
      Of woods and whispering wind.
Whether 'tis Spring's first shiver, faintly heard
  Through the light leaves, or lizards in the brake
    The rustling thorns have stirr'd,
      Her heart, her knees, they quake.
Yet I, who chase you, no grim lion am,
  No tiger fell, to crush you in my gripe:
    Come, learn to leave your dam,
      For lover's kisses ripe.

XXIV.

QUIS DESIDERIO.

Why blush to let our tears unmeasured fall
  For one so dear? Begin the mournful stave,
Melpomene, to whom the Sire of all
    Sweet voice with music gave.
And sleeps he then the heavy sleep of death,
  Quintilius? Piety, twin sister dear
Of Justice! naked Truth! unsullied Faith!
    When will ye find his peer?
By many a good man wept. Quintilius dies;
  By none than you, my Virgil, trulier wept:
Devout in vain, you chide the faithless skies,
    Asking your loan ill-kept.
No, though more suasive than the bard of Thrace
  You swept the lyre that trees were fain to hear,
Ne'er should the blood revisit his pale face
    Whom once with wand severe
Mercury has folded with the sons of night,
  Untaught to prayer Fate's prison to unseal.
Ah, heavy grief! but patience makes more light
    What sorrow may not heal.

XXVI.

MUSIS AMICUS.

The Muses love me: fear and grief,
  The winds may blow them to the sea;
Who quail before the wintry chief
  Of Scythia's realm, is nought to me.
What cloud o'er Tiridates lowers,
  I care not, I. O, nymph divine
Of virgin springs, with sunniest flowers
  A chaplet for my Lamia twine,
Pimplea sweet! my praise were vain
  Without thee. String this maiden lyre,
Attune for him the Lesbian strain,
  O goddess, with thy sister quire!

XXVII.

NATIS IN USUM.

What, fight with cups that should give joy?
  'Tis barbarous; leave such savage ways
To Thracians. Bacchus, shamefaced boy,
  Is blushing at your bloody frays.
The Median sabre! lights and wine!
  Was stranger contrast ever seen?
Cease, cease this brawling, comrades mine,
  And still upon your elbows lean.
Well, shall I take a toper's part
  Of fierce Falernian? let our guest,
Megilla's brother, say what dart
  Gave the death-wound that makes him blest.
He hesitates? no other hire
  Shall tempt my sober brains. Whate'er
The goddess tames you, no base fire
  She kindles; 'tis some gentle fair
Allures you still. Come, tell me truth,
  And trust my honour.—That the name?
That wild Charybdis yours? Poor youth!
  O, you deserved a better flame!
What wizard, what Thessalian spell,
  What god can save you, hamper'd thus?
To cope with this Chimaera fell
  Would task another Pegasus.

XXVIII.

TE MARIS ET TERRA.

The sea, the earth, the innumerable sand,
  Archytas, thou couldst measure; now, alas!
A little dust on Matine shore has spann'd
  That soaring spirit; vain it was to pass
The gates of heaven, and send thy soul in quest
  O'er air's wide realms; for thou hadst yet to die.
Ay, dead is Pelops' father, heaven's own guest,
  And old Tithonus, rapt from earth to sky,
And Minos, made the council-friend of Jove;
  And Panthus' son has yielded up his breath
Once more, though down he pluck'd the shield, to prove
  His prowess under Troy, and bade grim death
O'er skin and nerves alone exert its power,
  Not he, you grant, in nature meanly read.
Yes, all "await the inevitable hour;"
  The downward journey all one day must tread.
Some bleed, to glut the war-god's savage eyes;
  Fate meets the sailor from the hungry brine;
Youth jostles age in funeral obsequies;
  Each brow in turn is touch'd by Proserpine.
Me, too, Orion's mate, the Southern blast,
  Whelm'd in deep death beneath the Illyrian wave.
But grudge not, sailor, of driven sand to cast
  A handful on my head, that owns no grave.
So, though the eastern tempests loudly threat
  Hesperia's main, may green Venusia's crown
Be stripp'd, while you lie warm; may blessings yet
  Stream from Tarentum's guard, great Neptune, down,
And gracious Jove, into your open lap!
  What! shrink you not from crime whose punishment
Falls on your innocent children? it may hap
  Imperious Fate will make yourself repent.
My prayers shall reach the avengers of all wrong;
  No expiations shall the curse unbind.
Great though your haste, I would not task you long;
  Thrice sprinkle dust, then scud before the wind.

XXIX.

ICCI, BEATIS.

Your heart on Arab wealth is set,
  Good Iccius: you would try your steel
On Saba's kings, unconquer'd yet,

And make the Mede your fetters feel.
Come, tell me what barbarian fair
  Will serve you now, her bridegroom slain?
What page from court with essenced hair
  Will tender you the bowl you drain,
Well skill'd to bend the Serian bow
  His father carried? Who shall say
That rivers may not uphill flow,
  And Tiber's self return one day,
If you would change Panaetius' works,
  That costly purchase, and the clan
Of Socrates, for shields and dirks,
  Whom once we thought a saner man?

XXX.

O VENUS.

Come, Cnidian, Paphian Venus, come,
  Thy well-beloved Cyprus spurn,
Haste, where for thee in Glycera's home
  Sweet odours burn.
Bring too thy Cupid, glowing warm,
  Graces and Nymphs, unzoned and free,
And Youth, that lacking thee lacks charm,
  And Mercury.

XXXI.

QUID DEDICATUM.

What blessing shall the bard entreat
  The god he hallows, as he pours
The winecup? Not the mounds of wheat
  That load Sardinian threshing floors;
Not Indian gold or ivory—no,
  Nor flocks that o'er Calabria stray,
Nor fields that Liris, still and slow,
  Is eating, unperceived, away.
Let those whose fate allows them train
  Calenum's vine; let trader bold
From golden cups rich liquor drain
  For wares of Syria bought and sold,

Heaven's favourite, sooth, for thrice a-year
  He comes and goes across the brine
Undamaged. I in plenty here
  On endives, mallows, succory dine.
O grant me, Phoebus, calm content,
  Strength unimpair'd, a mind entire,
Old age without dishonour spent,
  Nor unbefriended by the lyre!

XXXII.

POSCIMUR.

They call;—if aught in shady dell
  We twain have warbled, to remain
Long months or years, now breathe, my shell,
   A Roman strain,
Thou, strung by Lesbos' minstrel hand,
  The bard, who 'mid the clash of steel,
Or haply mooring to the strand
   His batter'd keel,
Of Bacchus and the Muses sung,
  And Cupid, still at Venus' side,
And Lycus, beautiful and young,
   Dark-hair'd, dark-eyed.
O sweetest lyre, to Phoebus dear,
  Delight of Jove's high festival,
Blest balm in trouble, hail and hear
   Whene'er I call!

XXXIII.

ALBI, NE DOLEAS.

What, Albius! why this passionate despair
  For cruel Glycera? why melt your voice
In dolorous strains, because the perjured fair
   Has made a younger choice?
See, narrow-brow'd Lycoris, how she glows
  For Cyrus! Cyrus turns away his head
To Pholoe's frown; but sooner gentle roes
   Apulian wolves shall wed,
Than Pholoe to so mean a conqueror strike:

So Venus wills it; 'neath her brazen yoke
She loves to couple forms and minds unlike,
    All for a heartless joke.
For me sweet Love had forged a milder spell;
   But Myrtale still kept me her fond slave,
More stormy she than the tempestuous swell
    That crests Calabria's wave.

XXXIV.

PARCUS DEORUM.

My prayers were scant, my offerings few,
  While witless wisdom fool'd my mind;
But now I trim my sails anew,
  And trace the course I left behind.
For lo! the Sire of heaven on high,
  By whose fierce bolts the clouds are riven,
To-day through an unclouded sky
  His thundering steeds and car has driven.
E'en now dull earth and wandering floods,
  And Atlas' limitary range,
And Styx, and Taenarus' dark abodes
  Are reeling. He can lowliest change
And loftiest; bring the mighty down
  And lift the weak; with whirring flight
Comes Fortune, plucks the monarch's crown,
  And decks therewith some meaner wight.

XXXV.

O DIVA, GRATUM.

Lady of Antium, grave and stern!
  O Goddess, who canst lift the low
To high estate, and sudden turn
  A triumph to a funeral show!
Thee the poor hind that tills the soil
  Implores; their queen they own in thee,
Who in Bithynian vessel toil
  Amid the vex'd Carpathian sea.
Thee Dacians fierce, and Scythian hordes,
  Peoples and towns, and Koine, their head,

And mothers of barbarian lords,
  And tyrants in their purple dread,
Lest, spurn'd by thee in scorn, should fall
  The state's tall prop, lest crowds on fire
To arms, to arms! the loiterers call,
  And thrones be tumbled in the mire.
Necessity precedes thee still
  With hard fierce eyes and heavy tramp:
Her hand the nails and wedges fill,
  The molten lead and stubborn clamp.
Hope, precious Truth in garb of white,
  Attend thee still, nor quit thy side
When with changed robes thou tak'st thy flight
  In anger from the homes of pride.
Then the false herd, the faithless fair,
  Start backward; when the wine runs dry,
The jocund guests, too light to bear
  An equal yoke, asunder fly.
O shield our Caesar as he goes
  To furthest Britain, and his band,
Rome's harvest! Send on Eastern foes
  Their fear, and on the Red Sea strand!
O wounds that scarce have ceased to run!
  O brother's blood! O iron time!
What horror have we left undone?
  Has conscience shrunk from aught of crime?
What shrine has rapine held in awe?
  What altar spared? O haste and beat
The blunted steel we yet may draw
  On Arab and on Massagete!

XXXVI.

ET THURE, ET FIDIBUS.

  Bid the lyre and cittern play;
Enkindle incense, shed the victim's gore;
  Heaven has watch'd o'er Numida,
And brings him safe from far Hispania's shore.
  Now, returning, he bestows
On each, dear comrade all the love he can;
  But to Lamia most he owes,
By whose sweet side he grew from boy to man.
  Note we in our calendar
This festal day with whitest mark from Crete:
  Let it flow, the old wine-jar,
And ply to Salian time your restless feet.
  Damalis tosses off her wine,
But Bassus sure must prove her match to-night.

Give us roses all to twine,
And parsley green, and lilies deathly white.
     Every melting eye will rest
On Damalis' lovely face; but none may part
     Damalis from our new-found guest;
She clings, and clings, like ivy, round his heart.

XXXVII.

NUNC EST BIBENDUM.

Now drink we deep, now featly tread
     A measure; now before each shrine
With Salian feasts the table spread;
     The time invites us, comrades mine.
'Twas shame to broach, before to-day,
     The Caecuban, while Egypt's dame
Threaten'd our power in dust to lay
     And wrap the Capitol in flame,
Girt with her foul emasculate throng,
     By Fortune's sweet new wine befool'd,
In hope's ungovern'd weakness strong
     To hope for all; but soon she cool'd,
To see one ship from burning 'scape;
     Great Caesar taught her dizzy brain,
Made mad by Mareotic grape,
     To feel the sobering truth of pain,
And gave her chase from Italy,
     As after doves fierce falcons speed,
As hunters 'neath Haemonia's sky
     Chase the tired hare, so might he lead
The fiend enchain'd; SHE sought to die
     More nobly, nor with woman's dread
Quail'd at the steel, nor timorously
     In her fleet ships to covert fled.
Amid her ruin'd halls she stood
     Unblench'd, and fearless to the end
Grasp'd the fell snakes, that all her blood
     Might with the cold black venom blend,
Death's purpose flushing in her face;
     Nor to our ships the glory gave,
That she, no vulgar dame, should grace
     A triumph, crownless, and a slave.

XXXVIII.

PERSICOS ODI.

No Persian cumber, boy, for me;
   I hate your garlands linden-plaited;
Leave winter's rose where on the tree
   It hangs belated.
Wreath me plain myrtle; never think
   Plain myrtle either's wear unfitting,
Yours as you wait, mine as I drink
   In vine-bower sitting.

BOOK II.

I.

MOTUM EX METELLO.

The broils that from Metellus date,
   The secret springs, the dark intrigues,
The freaks of Fortune, and the great
   Confederate in disastrous leagues,
And arms with uncleansed slaughter red,
   A work of danger and distrust,
You treat, as one on fire should tread,
   Scarce hid by treacherous ashen crust.
Let Tragedy's stern muse be mute
   Awhile; and when your order'd page
Has told Rome's tale, that buskin'd foot
   Again shall mount the Attic stage,
Pollio, the pale defendant's shield,
   In deep debate the senate's stay,
The hero of Dalmatic field
   By Triumph crown'd with deathless bay.
E'en now with trumpet's threatening blare
   You thrill our ears; the clarion brays;
The lightnings of the armour scare
   The steed, and daunt the rider's gaze.
Methinks I hear of leaders proud
   With no uncomely dust distain'd,
And all the world by conquest bow'd,
   And only Cato's soul unchain'd.
Yes, Juno and the powers on high
   That left their Afric to its doom,

Have led the victors' progeny
  As victims to Jugurtha's tomb.
What field, by Latian blood-drops fed,
  Proclaims not the unnatural deeds
It buries, and the earthquake dread
  Whose distant thunder shook the Medes?
What gulf, what river has not seen
  Those sights of sorrow? nay, what sea
Has Daunian carnage yet left green?
  What coast from Roman blood is free?
But pause, gay Muse, nor leave your play
  Another Cean dirge to sing;
With me to Venus' bower away,
  And there attune a lighter string.

II.

NULLUS ARGENTO.

The silver, Sallust, shows not fair
  While buried in the greedy mine:
You love it not till moderate wear
    Have given it shine.
Honour to Proculeius! he
  To brethren play'd a father's part;
Fame shall embalm through years to be
    That noble heart.
Who curbs a greedy soul may boast
  More power than if his broad-based throne
Bridged Libya's sea, and either coast
    Were all his own.
Indulgence bids the dropsy grow;
  Who fain would quench the palate's flame
Must rescue from the watery foe
    The pale weak frame.
Phraates, throned where Cyrus sate,
  May count for blest with vulgar herds,
But not with Virtue; soon or late
    From lying words
She weans men's lips; for him she keeps
  The crown, the purple, and the bays,
Who dares to look on treasure-heaps
    With unblench'd gaze.

III.

AEQUAM, MEMENTO.

An equal mind, when storms o'ercloud,
  Maintain, nor 'neath a brighter sky
Let pleasure make your heart too proud,
  O Dellius, Dellius! sure to die,
Whether in gloom you spend each year,
  Or through long holydays at ease
In grassy nook your spirit cheer
  With old Falernian vintages,
Where poplar pale, and pine-tree high
  Their hospitable shadows spread
Entwined, and panting waters try
  To hurry down their zigzag bed.
Bring wine and scents, and roses' bloom,
  Too brief, alas! to that sweet place,
While life, and fortune, and the loom
  Of the Three Sisters yield you grace.
Soon must you leave the woods you buy,
  Your villa, wash'd by Tiber's flow,
Leave,—and your treasures, heap'd so high,
  Your reckless heir will level low.
Whether from Argos' founder born
  In wealth you lived beneath the sun,
Or nursed in beggary and scorn,
  You fall to Death, who pities none.
One way all travel; the dark urn
  Shakes each man's lot, that soon or late
Will force him, hopeless of return,
  On board the exile-ship of Fate.

IV.

NE SIT ANCILLAE

Why, Xanthias, blush to own you love
  Your slave? Briseis, long ago,
A captive, could Achilles move
    With breast of snow.
Tecmessa's charms enslaved her lord,
  Stout Ajax, heir of Telamon;
Atrides, in his pride, adored
    The maid he won,

When Troy to Thessaly gave way,
  And Hector's all too quick decease
Made Pergamus an easier prey
    To wearied Greece.
What if, as auburn Phyllis' mate,
  You graft yourself on regal stem?
Oh yes! be sure her sires were great;
    She weeps for THEM.
Believe me, from no rascal scum
  Your charmer sprang; so true a flame,
Such hate of greed, could never come
    From vulgar dame.
With honest fervour I commend
  Those lips, those eyes; you need not fear
A rival, hurrying on to end
    His fortieth year.

VI.

SEPTIMI, GADES.

Septimius, who with me would brave
  Far Gades, and Cantabrian land
Untamed by Home, and Moorish wave
    That whirls the sand;
Fair Tibur, town of Argive kings,
  There would I end my days serene,
At rest from seas and travellings,
    And service seen.
Should angry Fate those wishes foil,
  Then let me seek Galesus, sweet
To skin-clad sheep, and that rich soil,
    The Spartan's seat.
O, what can match the green recess,
  Whose honey not to Hybla yields,
Whose olives vie with those that bless
    Venafrum's fields?
Long springs, mild winters glad that spot
  By Jove's good grace, and Aulon, dear
To fruitful Bacchus, envies not
    Falernian cheer.
That spot, those happy heights desire
  Our sojourn; there, when life shall end,
Your tear shall dew my yet warm pyre,
    Your bard and friend.

VII.

O SAEPE MECUM.

O, Oft with me in troublous time
  Involved, when Brutus warr'd in Greece,
Who gives you back to your own clime
  And your own gods, a man of peace,
Pompey, the earliest friend I knew,
  With whom I oft cut short the hours
With wine, my hair bright bathed in dew
  Of Syrian oils, and wreathed with flowers?
With you I shared Philippi's rout,
  Unseemly parted from my shield,
When Valour fell, and warriors stout
  Were tumbled on the inglorious field:
But I was saved by Mercury,
  Wrapp'd in thick mist, yet trembling sore,
While you to that tempestuous sea
  Were swept by battle's tide once more.
Come, pay to Jove the feast you owe;
  Lay down those limbs, with warfare spent,
Beneath my laurel; nor be slow
  To drain my cask; for you 'twas meant.
Lethe's true draught is Massic wine;
  Fill high the goblet; pour out free
Rich streams of unguent. Who will twine
  The hasty wreath from myrtle-tree
Or parsley? Whom will Venus seat
  Chairman of cups? Are Bacchants sane?
Then I'll be sober. O, 'tis sweet
  To fool, when friends come home again!

VIII.

ULLA SI JURIS.

Had chastisement for perjured truth,
  Barine, mark'd you with a curse—
Did one wry nail, or one black tooth,
    But make you worse—
I'd trust you; but, when plighted lies
  Have pledged you deepest, lovelier far
You sparkle forth, of all young eyes
    The ruling star.

'Tis gain to mock your mother's bones,
  And night's still signs, and all the sky,
And gods, that on their glorious thrones
    Chill Death defy.
Ay, Venus smiles; the pure nymphs smile,
  And Cupid, tyrant-lord of hearts,
Sharpening on bloody stone the while
    His fiery darts.
New captives fill the nets you weave;
  New slaves are bred; and those before,
Though oft they threaten, never leave
    Your godless door.
The mother dreads you for her son,
  The thrifty sire, the new-wed bride,
Lest, lured by you, her precious one
    Should leave her side.

IX.

NON SEMPER IMBRES.

The rain, it rains not every day
  On the soak'd meads; the Caspian main
Not always feels the unequal sway
  Of storms, nor on Armenia's plain,
Dear Valgius, lies the cold dull snow
  Through all the year; nor northwinds keen
Upon Garganian oakwoods blow,
  And strip the ashes of their green.
You still with tearful tones pursue
  Your lost, lost Mystes; Hesper sees
Your passion when he brings the dew,
  And when before the sun he flees.
Yet not for loved Antilochus
  Grey Nestor wasted all his years
In grief; nor o'er young Troilus
  His parents' and his sisters' tears
For ever flow'd. At length have done
  With these soft sorrows; rather tell
Of Caesar's trophies newly won,
  And hoar Niphates' icy fell,
And Medus' flood, 'mid conquer'd tribes
  Rolling a less presumptuous tide,
And Scythians taught, as Rome prescribes,
  Henceforth o'er narrower steppes to ride.

X.

RECTIUS VIVES.

Licinius, trust a seaman's lore:
  Steer not too boldly to the deep,
Nor, fearing storms, by treacherous shore
   Too closely creep.
Who makes the golden mean his guide,
  Shuns miser's cabin, foul and dark,
Shuns gilded roofs, where pomp and pride
   Are envy's mark.
With fiercer blasts the pine's dim height
  Is rock'd; proud towers with heavier fall
Crash to the ground; and thunders smite
   The mountains tall.
In sadness hope, in gladness fear
  'Gainst coming change will fortify
Your breast. The storms that Jupiter
   Sweeps o'er the sky
He chases. Why should rain to-day
  Bring rain to-morrow? Python's foe
Is pleased sometimes his lyre to play,
   Nor bends his bow.
Be brave in trouble; meet distress
  With dauntless front; but when the gale
Too prosperous blows, be wise no less,
   And shorten sail.

XI.

QUID BELLICOSUS.

O, Ask not what those sons of war,
  Cantabrian, Scythian, each intend,
Disjoin'd from us by Hadria's bar,
  Nor puzzle, Quintius, how to spend
A life so simple. Youth removes,
  And Beauty too; and hoar Decay
Drives out the wanton tribe of Loves
  And Sleep, that came or night or day.
The sweet spring-flowers not always keep
  Their bloom, nor moonlight shines the same
Each evening. Why with thoughts too deep
  O'ertask a mind of mortal frame?

Why not, just thrown at careless ease
  'Neath plane or pine, our locks of grey
Perfumed with Syrian essences
  And wreathed with roses, while we may,
Lie drinking? Bacchus puts to shame
  The cares that waste us. Where's the slave
To quench the fierce Falernian's flame
  With water from the passing wave?
Who'll coax coy Lyde from her home?
  Go, bid her take her ivory lyre,
The runaway, and haste to come,
  Her wild hair bound with Spartan tire.

XII.

NOLIS LONGA FERAE.

The weary war where fierce Numantia bled,
  Fell Hannibal, the swoln Sicilian main
Purpled with Punic blood—not mine to wed
    These to the lyre's soft strain,
Nor cruel Lapithae, nor, mad with wine,
  Centaurs, nor, by Herculean arm o'ercome,
The earth-born youth, whose terrors dimm'd the shine
    Of the resplendent dome
Of ancient Saturn. You, Maecenas, best
  In pictured prose of Caesar's warrior feats
Will tell, and captive kings with haughty crest
    Led through the Roman streets.
On me the Muse has laid her charge to tell
  Of your Licymnia's voice, the lustrous hue
Of her bright eye, her heart that beats so well
    To mutual passion true:
How nought she does but lends her added grace,
  Whether she dance, or join in bantering play,
Or with soft arms the maiden choir embrace
    On great Diana's day.
Say, would you change for all the wealth possest
  By rich Achaemenes or Phrygia's heir,
Or the full stores of Araby the blest,
    One lock of her dear hair,
While to your burning lips she bends her neck,
  Or with kind cruelty denies the due
She means you not to beg for, but to take,
    Or snatches it from you?

XIII.

ILLE ET NEFASTO.

Black day he chose for planting thee,
  Accurst he rear'd thee from the ground,
The bane of children yet to be,
  The scandal of the village round.
His father's throat the monster press'd
  Beside, and on his hearthstone spilt,
I ween, the blood of midnight guest;
  Black Colchian drugs, whate'er of guilt
Is hatch'd on earth, he dealt in all—
  Who planted in my rural stead
Thee, fatal wood, thee, sure to fall
  Upon thy blameless master's head.
The dangers of the hour! no thought
  We give them; Punic seaman's fear
Is all of Bosporus, nor aught
  Recks he of pitfalls otherwhere;
The soldier fears the mask'd retreat
  Of Parthia; Parthia dreads the thrall
Of Rome; but Death with noiseless feet
  Has stolen and will steal on all.
How near dark Pluto's court I stood,
  And AEacus' judicial throne,
The blest seclusion of the good,
  And Sappho, with sweet lyric moan
Bewailing her ungentle sex,
  And thee, Alcaeus, louder far
Chanting thy tale of woful wrecks,
  Of woful exile, woful war!
In sacred awe the silent dead
  Attend on each: but when the song
Of combat tells and tyrants fled,
  Keen ears, press'd shoulders, closer throng.
What marvel, when at those sweet airs
  The hundred-headed beast spell-bound
Each black ear droops, and Furies' hairs
  Uncoil their serpents at the sound?
Prometheus too and Pelops' sire
  In listening lose the sense of woe;
Orion hearkens to the lyre,
  And lets the lynx and lion go.

XIV.

EHEU, FUGACES.

Ah, Postumus! they fleet away,
  Our years, nor piety one hour
Can win from wrinkles and decay,
  And Death's indomitable power;
Not though three hundred bullocks flame
  Each year, to soothe the tearless king
Who holds huge Geryon's triple frame
  And Tityos in his watery ring,
That circling flood, which all must stem,
  Who eat the fruits that Nature yields,
Wearers of haughtiest diadem,
  Or humblest tillers of the fields.
In vain we shun war's contact red
  Or storm-tost spray of Hadrian main:
In vain, the season through, we dread
  For our frail lives Scirocco's bane.
Cocytus' black and stagnant ooze
  Must welcome you, and Danaus' seed
Ill-famed, and ancient Sisyphus
  To never-ending toil decreed.
Your land, your house, your lovely bride
  Must lose you; of your cherish'd trees
None to its fleeting master's side
  Will cleave, but those sad cypresses.
Your heir, a larger soul, will drain
  The hundred-padlock'd Caecuban,
And richer spilth the pavement stain
  Than e'er at pontiff's supper ran.

XV.

JAM PAUCA ARATRO.

Few roods of ground the piles we raise
  Will leave to plough; ponds wider spread
Than Lucrine lake will meet the gaze
  On every side; the plane unwed
Will top the elm; the violet-bed,
  The myrtle, each delicious sweet,
On olive-grounds their scent will shed,
  Where once were fruit-trees yielding meat;
Thick bays will screen the midday range
  Of fiercest suns. Not such the rule
Of Romulus, and Cato sage,

And all the bearded, good old school.
Each Roman's wealth was little worth,
  His country's much; no colonnade
For private pleasance wooed the North
  With cool "prolixity of shade."
None might the casual sod disdain
  To roof his home; a town alone,
At public charge, a sacred fane
  Were honour'd with the pomp of stone.

XVI.

OTIUM DIVOS.

For ease, in wide Aegean caught,
  The sailor prays, when clouds are hiding
The moon, nor shines of starlight aught
    For seaman's guiding:
For ease the Mede, with quiver gay:
  For ease rude Thrace, in battle cruel:
Can purple buy it, Grosphus? Nay,
    Nor gold, nor jewel.
No pomp, no lictor clears the way
  'Mid rabble-routs of troublous feelings,
Nor quells the cares that sport and play
    Round gilded ceilings.
More happy he whose modest board
  His father's well-worn silver brightens;
No fear, nor lust for sordid hoard,
    His light sleep frightens.
Why bend our bows of little span?
  Why change our homes for regions under
Another sun? What exiled man
    From self can sunder?
Care climbs the bark, and trims the sail,
  Curst fiend! nor troops of horse can 'scape her,
More swift than stag, more swift than gale
    That drives the vapour.
Blest in the present, look not forth
  On ills beyond, but soothe each bitter
With slow, calm smile. No suns on earth
    Unclouded glitter.
Achilles' light was quench'd at noon;
  A long decay Tithonus minish'd;
My hours, it may be, yet will run
    When yours are finish'd.
For you Sicilian heifers low,

Bleat countless flocks; for you are neighing
Proud coursers; Afric purples glow
  For your arraying
With double dyes; a small domain,
  The soul that breathed in Grecian harping,
My portion these; and high disdain
  Of ribald carping.

XVII.

CUR ME QUERELIS.

Why rend my heart with that sad sigh?
  It cannot please the gods or me
That you, Maecenas, first should die,
  My pillar of prosperity.
Ah! should I lose one half my soul
  Untimely, can the other stay
Behind it? Life that is not whole,
  Is THAT as sweet? The self-same day
Shall crush us twain; no idle oath
  Has Horace sworn; whene'er you go,
We both will travel, travel both
  The last dark journey down below.
No, not Chimaera's fiery breath,
  Nor Gyas, could he rise again,
Shall part us; Justice, strong as death,
  So wills it; so the Fates ordain.
Whether 'twas Libra saw me born
  Or angry Scorpio, lord malign
Of natal hour, or Capricorn,
  The tyrant of the western brine,
Our planets sure with concord strange
  Are blended. You by Jove's blest power
Were snatch'd from out the baleful range
  Of Saturn, and the evil hour
Was stay'd, when rapturous benches full
  Three times the auspicious thunder peal'd;
Me the curst trunk, that smote my skull,
  Had slain; but Faunus, strong to shield
The friends of Mercury, check'd the blow
  In mid descent. Be sure to pay
The victims and the fane you owe;
  Your bard a humbler lamb will slay.

XVIII.

NON EBUR.

Carven ivory have I none;
No golden cornice in my dwelling shines;
　　Pillars choice of Libyan stone
Upbear no architrave from Attic mines;
　　'Twas not mine to enter in
To Attalus' broad realms, an unknown heir,
　　Nor for me fair clients spin
Laconian purples for their patron's wear.
　　Truth is mine, and Genius mine;
The rich man comes, and knocks at my low door:
　　Favour'd thus, I ne'er repine,
Nor weary out indulgent Heaven for more:
　　In my Sabine homestead blest,
Why should I further tax a generous friend?
　　Suns are hurrying suns a-west,
And newborn moons make speed to meet their end.
　　You have hands to square and hew
Vast marble-blocks, hard on your day of doom,
　　Ever building mansions new,
Nor thinking of the mansion of the tomb.
　　Now you press on ocean's bound,
Where waves on Baiae beat, as earth were scant;
　　Now absorb your neighbour's ground,
And tear his landmarks up, your own to plant.
　　Hedges set round clients' farms
Your avarice tramples; see, the outcasts fly,
　　Wife and husband, in their arms
Their fathers' gods, their squalid family.
　　Yet no hall that wealth e'er plann'd
Waits you more surely than the wider room
　　Traced by Death's yet greedier hand.
Why strain so far? you cannot leap the tomb.
　　Earth removes the impartial sod
Alike for beggar and for monarch's child:
　　Nor the slave of Hell's dark god
Convey'd Prometheus back, with bribe beguiled.
　　Pelops he and Pelops' sire
Holds, spite of pride, in close captivity;
　　Beggars, who of labour tire,
Call'd or uncall'd, he hears and sets them free.

XIX.

BACCHUM IN REMOTIS.

Bacchus I saw in mountain glades
  Retired (believe it, after years!)
Teaching his strains to Dryad maids,
  While goat-hoof'd satyrs prick'd their ears.
Evoe! my eyes with terror glare;
  My heart is revelling with the god;
'Tis madness! Evoe! spare, O spare,
  Dread wielder of the ivied rod!
Yes, I may sing the Thyiad crew,
  The stream of wine, the sparkling rills
That run with milk, and honey-dew
  That from the hollow trunk distils;
And I may sing thy consort's crown,
  New set in heaven, and Pentheus' hall
With ruthless ruin thundering down,
  And proud Lycurgus' funeral.
Thou turn'st the rivers, thou the sea;
  Thou, on far summits, moist with wine,
Thy Bacchants' tresses harmlessly
  Dost knot with living serpent-twine.
Thou, when the giants, threatening wrack,
  Were clambering up Jove's citadel,
Didst hurl o'erweening Rhoetus back,
  In tooth and claw a lion fell.
Who knew thy feats in dance and play
  Deem'd thee belike for war's rough game
Unmeet: but peace and battle-fray
  Found thee, their centre, still the same.
Grim Cerberus wagg'd his tail to see
  Thy golden horn, nor dream'd of wrong,
But gently fawning, follow'd thee,
  And lick'd thy feet with triple tongue.

XX.

NON USITATA.

No vulgar wing, nor weakly plied,
  Shall bear me through the liquid sky;
A two-form'd bard, no more to bide
  Within the range of envy's eye
'Mid haunts of men. I, all ungraced
  By gentle blood, I, whom you call
Your friend, Maecenas, shall not taste

Of death, nor chafe in Lethe's thrall.
E'en now a rougher skin expands
  Along my legs: above I change
To a white bird; and o'er my hands
  And shoulders grows a plumage strange:
Fleeter than Icarus, see me float
  O'er Bosporus, singing as I go,
And o'er Gastulian sands remote,
  And Hyperborean fields of snow;
By Dacian horde, that masks its fear
  Of Marsic steel, shall I be known,
And furthest Scythian: Spain shall hear
  My warbling, and the banks of Rhone.
No dirges for my fancied death;
  No weak lament, no mournful stave;
All clamorous grief were waste of breath,
  And vain the tribute of o grave.

BOOK III.

I.

ODI PROFANUM.

I bid the unhallow'd crowd avaunt!
  Keep holy silence; strains unknown
Till now, the Muses' hierophant,
  I sing to youths and maids alone.
Kings o'er their flocks the sceptre wield;
  E'en kings beneath Jove's sceptre bow:
Victor in giant battle-field,
  He moves all nature with his brow.
This man his planted walks extends
  Beyond his peers; an older name
One to the people's choice commends;
  One boasts a more unsullied fame;
One plumes him on a larger crowd
  Of clients. What are great or small?
Death takes the mean man with the proud;
  The fatal urn has room for all.
When guilty Pomp the drawn sword sees
  Hung o'er her, richest feasts in vain
Strain their sweet juice her taste to please;
  No lutes, no singing birds again
Will bring her sleep. Sleep knows no pride;
  It scorns not cots of village hinds,

Nor shadow-trembling river-side,
  Nor Tempe, stirr'd by western winds.
Who, having competence, has all,
  The tumult of the sea defies,
Nor fears Arcturus' angry fall,
  Nor fears the Kid-star's sullen rise,
Though hail-storms on the vineyard beat,
  Though crops deceive, though trees complain.
One while of showers, one while of heat,
  One while of winter's barbarous reign.
Fish feel the narrowing of the main
  From sunken piles, while on the strand
Contractors with their busy train
  Let down huge stones, and lords of land
Affect the sea: but fierce Alarm
  Can clamber to the master's side:
Black Cares can up the galley swarm,
  And close behind the horseman ride.
If Phrygian marbles soothe not pain,
  Nor star-bright purple's costliest wear,
Nor vines of true Falernian strain,
  Nor Achaemenian spices rare,
Why with rich gate and pillar'd range
  Upbuild new mansions, twice as high,
Or why my Sabine vale exchange
  For more laborious luxury?

II.

ANGUSTAM AMICE.

To suffer hardness with good cheer,
  In sternest school of warfare bred,
Our youth should learn; let steed and spear
  Make him one day the Parthian's dread;
Cold skies, keen perils, brace his life.
  Methinks I see from rampined town
Some battling tyrant's matron wife,
  Some maiden, look in terror down,—
"Ah, my dear lord, untrain'd in war!
  O tempt not the infuriate mood
Of that fell lion! see! from far
  He plunges through a tide of blood!"
What joy, for fatherland to die!
  Death's darts e'en flying feet o'ertake,
Nor spare a recreant chivalry,
  A back that cowers, or loins that quake.

True Virtue never knows defeat:
  HER robes she keeps unsullied still,
Nor takes, nor quits, HER curule seat
  To please a people's veering will.
True Virtue opens heaven to worth:
  She makes the way she does not find:
The vulgar crowd, the humid earth,
  Her soaring pinion leaves behind.
Seal'd lips have blessings sure to come:
  Who drags Eleusis' rite to day,
That man shall never share my home,
  Or join my voyage: roofs give way
And boats are wreck'd: true men and thieves
  Neglected Justice oft confounds:
Though Vengeance halt, she seldom leaves
  The wretch whose flying steps she hounds.

III.

JUSTUM ET TENACEM.

The man of firm and righteous will,
  No rabble, clamorous for the wrong,
No tyrant's brow, whose frown may kill,
  Can shake the strength that makes him strong:
Not winds, that chafe the sea they sway,
  Nor Jove's right hand, with lightning red:
Should Nature's pillar'd frame give way,
  That wreck would strike one fearless head.
Pollux and roving Hercules
  Thus won their way to Heaven's proud steep,
'Mid whom Augustus, couch'd at ease,
  Dyes his red lips with nectar deep.
For this, great Bacchus, tigers drew
  Thy glorious car, untaught to slave
In harness: thus Quirinus flew
  On Mars' wing'd steeds from Acheron's wave,
When Juno spoke with Heaven's assent:
  "O Ilium, Ilium, wretched town!
The judge accurst, incontinent,
  And stranger dame have dragg'd thee down.
Pallas and I, since Priam's sire
  Denied the gods his pledged reward,
Had doom'd them all to sword and fire,
  The people and their perjured lord.
No more the adulterous guest can charm
  The Spartan queen: the house forsworn

151

No more repels by Hector's arm
  My warriors, baffled and outworn:
Hush'd is the war our strife made long:
  I welcome now, my hatred o'er,
A grandson in the child of wrong,
  Him whom the Trojan priestess bore.
Receive him, Mars! the gates of flame
  May open: let him taste forgiven
The nectar, and enrol his name
  Among the peaceful ranks of Heaven.
Let the wide waters sever still
  Ilium and Rome, the exiled race
May reign and prosper where they will:
  So but in Paris' burial-place
The cattle sport, the wild beasts hide
  Their cubs, the Capitol may stand
All bright, and Rome in warlike pride
  O'er Media stretch a conqueror's hand.
Aye, let her scatter far and wide
  Her terror, where the land-lock'd waves
Europe from Afric's shore divide,
  Where swelling Nile the corn-field laves—
Of strength more potent to disdain
  Hid gold, best buried in the mine,
Than gather it with hand profane,
  That for man's greed would rob a shrine.
Whate'er the bound to earth ordain'd,
  There let her reach the arm of power,
Travelling, where raves the fire unrein'd,
  And where the storm-cloud and the shower.
Yet, warlike Roman, know thy doom,
  Nor, drunken with a conqueror's joy,
Or blind with duteous zeal, presume
  To build again ancestral Troy.
Should Troy revive to hateful life,
  Her star again should set in gore,
While I, Jove's sister and his wife,
  To victory led my host once more.
Though Phoebus thrice in brazen mail
  Should case her towers, they thrice should fall,
Storm'd by my Greeks: thrice wives should wail
  Husband and son, themselves in thrall."
—Such thunders from the lyre of love!
  Back, wayward Muse! refrain, refrain
To tell the talk of gods above,
  And dwarf high themes in puny strain.

IV.

Come down, Calliope, from above:
  Breathe on the pipe a strain of fire;
Or if a graver note thou love,
  With Phoebus' cittern and his lyre.
You hear her? or is this the play
  Of fond illusion? Hark! meseems
Through gardens of the good I stray,
  'Mid murmuring gales and purling streams.
Me, as I lay on Vultur's steep,
  A truant past Apulia's bound,
O'ertired, poor child, with play and sleep,
  With living green the stock-doves crown'd—
A legend, nay, a miracle,
  By Acherontia's nestlings told,
By all in Bantine glade that dwell,
  Or till the rich Forentan mould.
"Bears, vipers, spared him as he lay,
  The sacred garland deck'd his hair,
The myrtle blended with the bay:
  The child's inspired: the gods were there."
Your grace, sweet Muses, shields me still
  On Sabine heights, or lets me range
Where cool Praeneste, Tibur's hill,
  Or liquid Baiae proffers change.
Me to your springs, your dances true,
  Philippi bore not to the ground,
Nor the doom'd tree in falling slew,
  Nor billowy Palinurus drown'd.
Grant me your presence, blithe and fain
  Mad Bosporus shall my bark explore;
My foot shall tread the sandy plain
  That glows beside Assyria's shore;
'Mid Briton tribes, the stranger's foe,
  And Spaniards, drunk with horses' blood,
And quiver'd Scythians, will I go
  Unharm'd, and look on Tanais' flood.
When Caesar's self in peaceful town
  The weary veteran's home has made,
You bid him lay his helmet down
  And rest in your Pierian shade.
Mild thoughts you plant, and joy to see
  Mild thoughts take root. The nations know
How with descending thunder He
  The impious Titans hurl'd below,
Who rules dull earth and stormy seas,

And towns of men, and realms of pain,
And gods, and mortal companies,
  Alone, impartial in his reign.
Yet Jove had fear'd the giant rush,
  Their upraised arms, their port of pride,
And the twin brethren bent to push
  Huge Pelion up Olympus' side.
But Typhon, Mimas, what could these,
  Or what Porphyrion's stalwart scorn,
Rhoetus, or he whose spears were trees,
  Enceladus, from earth uptorn,
As on they rush'd in mad career
  'Gainst Pallas' shield? Here met the foe
Fierce Vulcan, queenly Juno here,
  And he who ne'er shall quit his bow,
Who laves in clear Castalian flood
  His locks, and loves the leafy growth
Of Lycia next his native wood,
  The Delian and the Pataran both.
Strength, mindless, falls by its own weight;
  Strength, mix'd with mind, is made more strong
By the just gods, who surely hate
  The strength whose thoughts are set on wrong.
Let hundred-handed Gyas bear
  His witness, and Orion known
Tempter of Dian, chaste and fair,
  By Dian's maiden dart o'erthrown.
Hurl'd on the monstrous shapes she bred,
  Earth groans, and mourns her children thrust
To Orcus; Aetna's weight of lead
  Keeps down the fire that breaks its crust;
Still sits the bird on Tityos' breast,
  The warder of unlawful love;
Still suffers lewd Pirithous, prest
  By massive chains no hand may move.

V.

CAELO TONANTEM.

Jove rules in heaven, his thunder shows;
  Henceforth Augustus earth shall own
Her present god, now Briton foes
  And Persians bow before his throne.
Has Crassus' soldier ta'en to wife
  A base barbarian, and grown grey
(Woe, for a nation's tainted life!)

Earning his foemen-kinsmen's pay,
  His king, forsooth, a Mede, his sire
    A Marsian? can he name forget,
  Gown, sacred shield, undying fire,
    And Jove and Rome are standing yet?
'Twas this that Regulus foresaw,
  What time he spurn'd the foul disgrace
Of peace, whose precedent would draw
  Destruction on an unborn race,
Should aught but death the prisoner's chain
  Unrivet. "I have seen," he said,
"Rome's eagle in a Punic fane,
  And armour, ne'er a blood-drop shed,
Stripp'd from the soldier; I have seen
  Free sons of Rome with arms fast tied;
The fields we spoil'd with corn are green,
  And Carthage opes her portals wide.
The warrior, sure, redeem'd by gold,
  Will fight the bolder! Aye, you heap
On baseness loss. The hues of old
  Revisit not the wool we steep;
And genuine worth, expell'd by fear,
  Returns not to the worthless slave.
Break but her meshes, will the deer
  Assail you? then will he be brave
Who once to faithless foes has knelt;
  Yes, Carthage yet his spear will fly,
Who with bound arms the cord has felt,
  The coward, and has fear'd to die.
He knows not, he, how life is won;
  Thinks war, like peace, a thing of trade!
Great art thou, Carthage! mate the sun,
  While Italy in dust is laid!"
His wife's pure kiss he waved aside,
  And prattling boys, as one disgraced,
They tell us, and with manly pride
  Stern on the ground his visage placed.
With counsel thus ne'er else aread
  He nerved the fathers' weak intent,
And, girt by friends that mourn'd him, sped
  Into illustrious banishment.
Well witting what the torturer's art
  Design'd him, with like unconcern
The press of kin he push'd apart
  And crowds encumbering his return,
As though, some tedious business o'er
  Of clients' court, his journey lay
Towards Venafrum's grassy floor,
  Or Sparta-built Tarentum's bay.

VI.

DELICTA MAJORUM.

Your fathers' guilt you still must pay,
  Till, Roman, you restore each shrine,
Each temple, mouldering in decay,
  And smoke-grimed statue, scarce divine.
Revering Heaven, you rule below;
  Be that your base, your coping still;
'Tis Heaven neglected bids o'erflow
  The measure of Italian ill.
Now Pacorus and Montaeses twice
  Have given our unblest arms the foil;
Their necklaces, of mean device,
  Smiling they deck with Roman spoil.
Our city, torn by faction's throes,
  Dacian and Ethiop well-nigh razed,
These with their dreadful navy, those
  For archer-prowess rather praised.
An evil age erewhile debased
  The marriage-bed, the race, the home;
Thence rose the flood whose waters waste
  The nation and the name of Rome.
Not such their birth, who stain'd for us
  The sea with Punic carnage red,
Smote Pyrrhus, smote Antiochus,
  And Hannibal, the Roman's dread.
Theirs was a hardy soldier-brood,
  Inured all day the land to till
With Sabine spade, then shoulder wood
  Hewn at a stern old mother's will,
When sunset lengthen'd from each height
  The shadows, and unyoked the steer,
Restoring in its westward flight
  The hour to toilworn travail dear.
What has not cankering Time made worse?
  Viler than grandsires, sires beget
Ourselves, yet baser, soon to curse
  The world with offspring baser yet.

VII.

QUID FLES, ASTERIE.

Why weep for him whom sweet Favonian airs
  Will waft next spring, Asteria, back to you,
    Rich with Bithynia's wares,
      A lover fond and true,
Your Gyges? He, detain'd by stormy stress
  At Oricum, about the Goat-star's rise,
    Cold, wakeful, comfortless,
      The long night weeping lies.
Meantime his lovesick hostess' messenger
  Talks of the flames that waste poor Chloe's heart
    (Flames lit for you, not her!)
      With a besieger's art;
Shows how a treacherous woman's lying breath
  Once on a time on trustful Proetus won
    To doom to early death
      Too chaste Bellerophon;
Warns him of Peleus' peril, all but slain
  For virtuous scorn of fair Hippolyta,
    And tells again each tale
      That e'er led heart astray.
In vain; for deafer than Icarian seas
  He hears, untainted yet. But, lady fair,
    What if Enipeus please
      Your listless eye? beware!
Though true it be that none with surer seat
  O'er Mars's grassy turf is seen to ride,
    Nor any swims so fleet
      Adown the Tuscan tide,
Yet keep each evening door and window barr'd;
  Look not abroad when music strikes up shrill,
    And though he call you hard,
      Remain obdurate still.

VIII.

MARTIIS COELEBS.

The first of March! a man unwed!
  What can these flowers, this censer
Or what these embers, glowing red
    On sods of green?
You ask, in either language skill'd!
  A feast I vow'd to Bacchus free,
A white he-goat, when all but kill'd
    By falling tree.
So, when that holyday comes round,
  It sees me still the rosin clear

From this my wine-jar, first embrown'd
  In Tullus' year.
Come, crush one hundred cups for life
 Preserved, Maecenas; keep till day
The candles lit; let noise and strife
  Be far away.
Lay down that load of state-concern;
 The Dacian hosts are all o'erthrown;
The Mede, that sought our overturn,
  Now seeks his own;
A servant now, our ancient foe,
 The Spaniard, wears at last our chain;
The Scythian half unbends his bow
  And quits the plain.
Then fret not lest the state should ail;
 A private man such thoughts may spare;
Enjoy the present hour's regale,
  And banish care.

IX.

DONEC GRATUS ERAM.

HORACE.
While I had power to bless you,
 Nor any round that neck his arms did fling
  More privileged to caress you,
Happier was Horace than the Persian king.

LYDIA. While you for none were pining
Sorer, nor Lydia after Chloe came,
  Lydia, her peers outshining,
Might match her own with Ilia's Roman fame.

H. Now Chloe is my treasure,
Whose voice, whose touch, can make sweet music flow:
  For her I'd die with pleasure,
Would Fate but spare the dear survivor so.

L. I love my own fond lover,
Young Calais, son of Thurian Ornytus:
  For him I'd die twice over,
Would Fate but spare the sweet survivor thus.

H. What now, if Love returning
Should pair us 'neath his brazen yoke once more,

And, bright-hair'd Chloe spurning,
Horace to off-cast Lydia ope his door?

L. Though he is fairer, milder,
Than starlight, you lighter than bark of tree,
   Than stormy Hadria wilder,
With you to live, to die, were bliss for me.

X.

EXTREMUM TANAIN.

Ah Lyce! though your drink were Tanais,
   Your husband some rude savage, you would weep
To leave me shivering, on a night like this,
   Where storms their watches keep.
Hark! how your door is creaking! how the grove
   In your fair court-yard, while the wild winds blow,
Wails in accord! with what transparence Jove
   Is glazing the driven snow!
Cease that proud temper: Venus loves it not:
   The rope may break, the wheel may backward turn:
Begetting you, no Tuscan sire begot
   Penelope the stern.
O, though no gift, no "prevalence of prayer,"
   Nor lovers' paleness deep as violet,
Nor husband, smit with a Pierian fair,
   Move you, have pity yet!
O harder e'en than toughest heart of oak,
   Deafer than uncharm'd snake to suppliant moans!
This side, I warn you, will not always brook
   Rain-water and cold stones.

XI.

MERCURI, NAM TE.

Come, Mercury, by whose minstrel spell
   Amphion raised the Theban stones,
Come, with thy seven sweet strings, my shell,
   Thy "diverse tones,"
Nor vocal once nor pleasant, now
   To rich man's board and temple dear:

Put forth thy power, till Lyde bow
    Her stubborn ear.
She, like a three year colt unbroke,
  Is frisking o'er the spacious plain,
Too shy to bear a lover's yoke,
    A husband's rein.
The wood, the tiger, at thy call
  Have follow'd: thou canst rivers stay:
The monstrous guard of Pluto's hall
    To thee gave way,
Grim Cerberus, round whose Gorgon head
  A hundred snakes are hissing death,
Whose triple jaws black venom shed,
    And sickening breath.
Ixion too and Tityos smooth'd
  Their rugged brows: the urn stood dry
One hour, while Danaus' maids were sooth'd
    With minstrelsy.
Let Lyde hear those maidens' guilt,
  Their famous doom, the ceaseless drain
Of outpour'd water, ever spilt,
    And all the pain
Reserved for sinners, e'en when dead:
  Those impious hands, (could crime do more?)
Those impious hands had hearts to shed
    Their bridegrooms' gore!
One only, true to Hymen's flame,
  Was traitress to her sire forsworn:
That splendid falsehood lights her name
    Through times unborn.
"Wake!" to her youthful spouse she cried,
  "Wake! or you yet may sleep too well:
Fly—from the father of your bride,
    Her sisters fell:
They, as she-lions bullocks rend,
  Tear each her victim: I, less hard
Than these, will slay you not, poor friend,
    Nor hold in ward:
Me let my sire in fetters lay
  For mercy to my husband shown:
Me let him ship far hence away,
    To climes unknown.
Go; speed your flight o'er land and wave,
  While Night and Venus shield you; go
Be blest: and on my tomb engrave
    This tale of woe."

XII.

MISERARUM EST.

How unhappy are the maidens who with Cupid may not play,
Who may never touch the wine-cup, but must tremble all the day
  At an uncle, and the scourging of his tongue!
Neobule, there's a robber takes your needle and your thread,
Lets the lessons of Minerva run no longer in your head;
  It is Hebrus, the athletic and the young!
O, to see him when anointed he is plunging in the flood!
What a seat he has on horseback! was Bellerophon's as good?
  As a boxer, as a runner, past compare!
When the deer are flying blindly all the open country o'er,
He can aim and he can hit them; he can steal upon the boar,
  As it couches in the thicket unaware.

XIII.

O FONS BANDUSIAE.

Bandusia's fount, in clearness crystalline,
  O worthy of the wine, the flowers we vow!
    To-morrow shall be thine
      A kid, whose crescent brow
Is sprouting all for love and victory.
  In vain: his warm red blood, so early stirr'd,
    Thy gelid stream shall dye,
      Child of the wanton herd.
Thee the fierce Sirian star, to madness fired,
  Forbears to touch: sweet cool thy waters yield
    To ox with ploughing tired,
      And lazy sheep afield.
Thou too one day shalt win proud eminence
  'Mid honour'd founts, while I the ilex sing
    Crowning the cavern, whence
      Thy babbling wavelets spring.

XIV.

HERCULIS RITU.

Our Hercules, they told us, Rome,
  Had sought the laurel Death bestows:
Now Glory brings him conqueror home
    From Spaniard foes.
Proud of her spouse, the imperial fair
  Must thank the gods that shield from death;
His sister too:—let matrons wear
    The suppliant wreath
For daughters and for sons restored:
  Ye youths and damsels newly wed,
Let decent awe restrain each word
    Best left unsaid.
This day, true holyday to me,
  Shall banish care: I will not fear
Rude broils or bloody death to see,
    While Caesar's here.
Quick, boy, the chaplets and the nard,
  And wine, that knew the Marsian war,
If roving Spartacus have spared
    A single jar.
And bid Nesera come and trill,
  Her bright locks bound with careless art:
If her rough porter cross your will,
    Why then depart.
Soon palls the taste for noise and fray,
  When hair is white and leaves are sere:
How had I fired in life's warm May,
    In Plancus' year!

XV.

UXOR PAUPERIS IBYCI.

  Wife of Ibycus the poor,
Let aged scandals have at length their bound:
  Give your graceless doings o'er,
Ripe as you are for going underground.
  YOU the maidens' dance to lead,
And cast your gloom upon those beaming stars!
  Daughter Pholoe may succeed,
But mother Chloris what she touches mars.
  Young men's homes your daughter storms,
Like Thyiad, madden'd by the cymbals' beat:
  Nothus' love her bosom warms:
She gambols like a fawn with silver feet.
  Yours should be the wool that grows
By fair Luceria, not the merry lute:

Flowers beseem not wither'd brows,
Nor wither'd lips with emptied wine-jars suit.

XVI.

INCLUSAM DANAEN.

Full well had Danae been secured, in truth,
  By oaken portals, and a brazen tower,
And savage watch-dogs, from the roving youth
    That prowl at midnight's hour:
But Jove and Venus mock'd with gay disdain
  The jealous warder of that close stronghold:
The way, they knew, must soon be smooth and plain
    When gods could change to gold.
Gold, gold can pass the tyrant's sentinel,
  Can shiver rocks with more resistless blow
Than is the thunder's. Argos' prophet fell,
    He and his house laid low,
And all for gain. The man of Macedon
  Cleft gates of cities, rival kings o'erthrew
By force of gifts: their cunning snares have won
    Rude captains and their crew.
As riches grow, care follows: men repine
  And thirst for more. No lofty crest I raise:
Wisdom that thought forbids, Maecenas mine,
    The knightly order's praise.
He that denies himself shall gain the more
  From bounteous Heaven. I strip me of my pride,
Desert the rich man's standard, and pass o'er
    To bare Contentment's side,
More proud as lord of what the great despise
  Than if the wheat thresh'd on Apulia's floor
I hoarded all in my huge granaries,
    'Mid vast possessions poor.
A clear fresh stream, a little field o'ergrown
  With shady trees, a crop that ne'er deceives,
Pass, though men know it not, their wealth, that own
    All Afric's golden sheaves.
Though no Calabrian bees their honey yield
  For me, nor mellowing sleeps the god of wine
In Formian jar, nor in Gaul's pasture-field
    The wool grows long and fine,
Yet Poverty ne'er comes to break my peace;
  If more I craved, you would not more refuse.
Desiring less, I better shall increase
    My tiny revenues,

Than if to Alyattes' wide domains
  I join'd the realms of Mygdon. Great desires
Sort with great wants. 'Tis best, when prayer obtains
    No more than life requires.

XVII.

AELI VETUSTO.

Aelius, of Lamus' ancient name
  (For since from that high parentage
The prehistoric Lamias came
  And all who fill the storied page,
No doubt you trace your line from him,
  Who stretch'd his sway o'er Formiae,
And Liris, whose still waters swim
  Where green Marica skirts the sea,
Lord of broad realms), an eastern gale
  Will blow to-morrow, and bestrew
The shore with weeds, with leaves the vale,
  If rain's old prophet tell me true,
The raven. Gather, while 'tis fine,
  Your wood; to-morrow shall be gay
With smoking pig and streaming wine,
  And lord and slave keep holyday.

XVIII.

FAUNE, NYMPHARUM.

O wont the flying Nymphs to woo,
  Good Faunus, through my sunny farm
Pass gently, gently pass, nor do
    My younglings harm.
Each year, thou know'st, a kid must die
  For thee; nor lacks the wine's full stream
To Venus' mate, the bowl; and high
    The altars steam.
Sure as December's nones appear,
  All o'er the grass the cattle play;
The village, with the lazy steer,
    Keeps holyday.
Wolves rove among the fearless sheep;

The woods for thee their foliage strow;
The delver loves on earth to leap,
    His ancient foe.

XIX.

QUANTUM DISTAT.

    What the time from Inachus
To Codrus, who in patriot battle fell,
    Who were sprung from Aeacus,
And how men fought at Ilion,—this you tell.
    What the wines of Chios cost,
Who with due heat our water can allay,
    What the hour, and who the host
To give us house-room,—this you will not say.
    Ho, there! wine to moonrise, wine
To midnight, wine to our new augur too!
    Nine to three or three to nine,
As each man pleases, makes proportion true.
    Who the uneven Muses loves,
Will fire his dizzy brain with three times three;
    Three once told the Grace approves;
She with her two bright sisters, gay and free,
    Shrinks, as maiden should, from strife:
But I'm for madness. What has dull'd the fire
    Of the Berecyntian fife?
Why hangs the flute in silence with the lyre?
    Out on niggard-handed boys!
Rain showers of roses; let old Lycus hear,
    Envious churl, our senseless noise,
And she, our neighbour, his ill-sorted fere.
    You with your bright clustering hair,
Your beauty, Telephus, like evening's sky,
    Rhoda loves, as young, as fair;
I for my Glycera slowly, slowly die.

XXI.

O NATE MECUM.

O born in Manlius' year with me,
    Whate'er you bring us, plaint or jest,

Or passion and wild revelry,
    Or, like a gentle wine-jar, rest;
Howe'er men call your Massic juice,
    Its broaching claims a festal day;
Come then; Corvinus bids produce
    A mellower wine, and I obey.
Though steep'd in all Socratic lore
    He will not slight you; do not fear.
They say old Cato o'er and o'er
    With wine his honest heart would cheer.
Tough wits to your mild torture yield
    Their treasures; you unlock the soul
Of wisdom and its stores conceal'd,
    Arm'd with Lyaeus' kind control.
'Tis yours the drooping heart to heal;
    Your strength uplifts the poor man's horn;
Inspired by you, the soldier's steel,
    The monarch's crown, he laughs to scorn.
Liber and Venus, wills she so,
    And sister Graces, ne'er unknit,
And living lamps shall see you flow
    Till stars before the sunrise flit.

XXII.

MONTIUM CUSTOS.

Guardian of hill and woodland, Maid,
    Who to young wives in childbirth's hour
Thrice call'd, vouchsafest sovereign aid,
        O three-form'd power!
This pine that shades my cot be thine;
    Here will I slay, as years come round,
A youngling boar, whose tusks design
        The side-long wound.

XXIII.

COELO SUPINAS.

If, Phidyle, your hands you lift
    To heaven, as each new moon is born,
Soothing your Lares with the gift

Of slaughter'd swine, and spice, and corn,
Ne'er shall Scirocco's bane assail
　Your vines, nor mildew blast your wheat,
Ne'er shall your tender younglings fail
　In autumn, when the fruits are sweet.
The destined victim 'mid the snows
　Of Algidus in oakwoods fed,
Or where the Alban herbage grows,
　Shall dye the pontiff's axes red;
No need of butcher'd sheep for you
　To make your homely prayers prevail;
Give but your little gods their due,
　The rosemary twined with myrtle frail.
The sprinkled salt, the votive meal,
　As soon their favour will regain,
Let but the hand be pure and leal,
　As all the pomp of heifers slain.

XXIV.

INTACTIS OPULENTIOR.

　Though your buried wealth surpass
The unsunn'd gold of Ind or Araby,
　Though with many a ponderous mass
You crowd the Tuscan and Apulian sea,
　Let Necessity but drive
Her wedge of adamant into that proud head,
　Vainly battling will you strive
To 'scape Death's noose, or rid your soul of dread.
　Better life the Scythians lead,
Trailing on waggon wheels their wandering home,
　Or the hardy Getan breed,
As o'er their vast unmeasured steppes they roam;
　Free the crops that bless their soil;
Their tillage wearies after one year's space;
　Each in turn fulfils his toil;
His period o'er, another takes his place.
　There the step-dame keeps her hand
From guilty plots, from blood of orphans clean;
　There no dowried wives command
Their feeble lords, or on adulterers lean.
　Theirs are dowries not of gold,
Their parents' worth, their own pure chastity,
　True to one, to others cold;
They dare not sin, or, if they dare, they die.
　O, whoe'er has heart and head

To stay our plague of blood, our civic brawls,
    Would he that his name be read
"Father of Rome" on lofty pedestals,
    Let him chain this lawless will,
And be our children's hero! cursed spite!
    Living worth we envy still,
Then seek it with strain'd eyes, when snatch'd from sight.
    What can sad laments avail
Unless sharp justice kill the taint of sin?
    What can laws, that needs must fail
Shorn of the aid of manners form'd within,
    If the merchant turns not back
From the fierce heats that round the tropic glow,
    Turns not from the regions black
With northern winds, and hard with frozen snow;
    Sailors override the wave,
While guilty poverty, more fear'd than vice,
    Bids us crime and suffering brave,
And shuns the ascent of virtue's precipice?
    Let the Capitolian fane,
The favour'd goal of yon vociferous crowd,
    Aye, or let the nearest main
Receive our gold, our jewels rich and proud:
    Slay we thus the cause of crime,
If yet we would repent and choose the good:
    Ours the task to take in time
This baleful lust, and crush it in the bud.
    Ours to mould our weakling sons
To nobler sentiment and manlier deed:
    Now the noble's first-born shuns
The perilous chase, nor learns to sit his steed:
    Set him to the unlawful dice,
Or Grecian hoop, how skilfully he plays!
    While his sire, mature in vice,
A friend, a partner, or a guest betrays,
    Hurrying, for an heir so base,
To gather riches. Money, root of ill,
    Doubt it not, still grows apace:
Yet the scant heap has somewhat lacking still.

XXV.

QUO ME, BACCHE.

    Whither, Bacchus, tear'st thou me,
Fill'd with thy strength? What dens, what forests these,
    Thus in wildering race I see?

What cave shall hearken to my melodies,
    Tuned to tell of Caesar's praise
And throne him high the heavenly ranks among?
    Sweet and strange shall be my lays,
A tale till now by poet voice unsung.
    As the Evian on the height,
Housed from her sleep, looks wonderingly abroad,
    Looks on Thrace with snow-drifts white,
And Rhodope by barbarous footstep trod,
    So my truant eyes admire
The banks, the desolate forests. O great King
    Who the Naiads dost inspire,
And Bacchants, strong from earth huge trees to wring!
    Not a lowly strain is mine,
No mere man's utterance. O, 'tis venture sweet
    Thee to follow, God of wine,
Making the vine-branch round thy temples meet!

XXVI.

VIRI PUELLIS.

For ladies's love I late was fit,
  And good success my warfare blest,
But now my arms, my lyre I quit,
  And hang them up to rust or rest.
Here, where arising from the sea
  Stands Venus, lay the load at last,
Links, crowbars, and artillery,
  Threatening all doors that dared be fast.
O Goddess! Cyprus owns thy sway,
  And Memphis, far from Thracian snow:
Raise high thy lash, and deal me, pray,
  That haughty Chloe just one blow!

XXVII.

IMPIOS PARRAE.

When guilt goes forth, let lapwings shrill,
  And dogs and foxes great with young,
And wolves from far Lanuvian hill,
    Give clamorous tongue:

Across the roadway dart the snake,
  Frightening, like arrow loosed from string,
The horses. I, for friendship's sake,
    Watching each wing,
Ere to his haunt, the stagnant marsh,
  The harbinger of tempest flies,
Will call the raven, croaking harsh,
    From eastern skies.
Farewell!—and wheresoe'er you go,
  My Galatea, think of me:
Let lefthand pie and roving crow
    Still leave you free.
But mark with what a front of fear
  Orion lowers. Ah! well I know
How Hadria glooms, how falsely clear
    The west-winds blow.
Let foemen's wives and children feel
  The gathering south-wind's angry roar,
The black wave's crash, the thunder-peal,
    The quivering shore.
So to the bull Europa gave
  Her beauteous form, and when she saw
The monstrous deep, the yawning grave,
    Grew pale with awe.
That morn of meadow-flowers she thought,
  Weaving a crown the nymphs to please:
That gloomy night she look'd on nought
    But stars and seas.
Then, as in hundred-citied Crete
  She landed,—"O my sire!" she said,
"O childly duty! passion's heat
    Has struck thee dead.
Whence came I? death, for maiden's shame,
  Were little. Do I wake to weep
My sin? or am I pure of blame,
    And is it sleep
From dreamland brings a form to trick
  My senses? Which was best? to go
Over the long, long waves, or pick
    The flowers in blow?
O, were that monster made my prize,
  How would I strive to wound that brow,
How tear those horns, my frantic eyes
    Adored but now!
Shameless I left my father's home;
  Shameless I cheat the expectant grave;
O heaven, that naked I might roam
    In lions' cave!
Now, ere decay my bloom devour
  Or thin the richness of my blood,

Fain would I fall in youth's first flower,
    The tigers' food.
Hark! 'tis my father—Worthless one!
  What, yet alive? the oak is nigh.
'Twas well you kept your maiden zone,
    The noose to tie.
Or if your choice be that rude pike,
  New barb'd with death, leap down and ask
The wind to bear you. Would you like
    The bondmaid's task,
You, child of kings, a master's toy,
  A mistress' slave?'" Beside her, lo!
Stood Venus smiling, and her boy
    With unstrung bow.
Then, when her laughter ceased, "Have done
  With fume and fret," she cried, "my fair;
That odious bull will give you soon
    His horns to tear.
You know not you are Jove's own dame:
  Away with sobbing; be resign'd
To greatness: you shall give your name
    To half mankind."

XXVIII.

FESTO QUID POTIUS.

Neptune's feast-day! what should man
  Think first of doing? Lyde mine, be bold,
  Broach the treasured Caecuban,
And batter Wisdom in her own stronghold.
  Now the noon has pass'd the full,
Yet sure you deem swift Time has made a halt,
  Tardy as you are to pull
Old Bibulus' wine-jar from its sleepy vault.
  I will take my turn and sing
Neptune and Nereus' train with locks of green;
  You shall warble to the string
Latona and her Cynthia's arrowy sheen.
  Hers our latest song, who sways
Cnidos and Cyclads, and to Paphos goes
  With her swans, on holydays;
Night too shall claim the homage music owes.

XXIX.

Heir of Tyrrhenian kings, for you
  A mellow cask, unbroach'd as yet,
Maecenas mine, and roses new,
  And fresh-drawn oil your locks to wet,
Are waiting here. Delay not still,
  Nor gaze on Tibur, never dried,
And sloping AEsule, and the hill
  Of Telegon the parricide.
O leave that pomp that can but tire,
  Those piles, among the clouds at home;
Cease for a moment to admire
  The smoke, the wealth, the noise of Rome!
In change e'en luxury finds a zest:
  The poor man's supper, neat, but spare,
With no gay couch to seat the guest,
  Has smooth'd the rugged brow of care.
Now glows the Ethiop maiden's sire;
  Now Procyon rages all ablaze;
The Lion maddens in his ire,
  As suns bring back the sultry days:
The shepherd with his weary sheep
  Seeks out the streamlet and the trees,
Silvanus' lair: the still banks sleep
  Untroubled by the wandering breeze.
You ponder on imperial schemes,
  And o'er the city's danger brood:
Bactrian and Serian haunt your dreams,
  And Tanais, toss'd by inward feud.
The issue of the time to be
  Heaven wisely hides in blackest night,
And laughs, should man's anxiety
  Transgress the bounds of man's short sight.
Control the present: all beside
  Flows like a river seaward borne,
Now rolling on its placid tide,
  Now whirling massy trunks uptorn,
And waveworn crags, and farms, and stock,
  In chaos blent, while hill and wood
Reverberate to the enormous shock,
  When savage rains the tranquil flood
Have stirr'd to madness. Happy he,
  Self-centred, who each night can say,
"My life is lived: the morn may see
  A clouded or a sunny day:
That rests with Jove: but what is gone,

He will not, cannot turn to nought;
Nor cancel, as a thing undone,
  What once the flying hour has brought."
Fortune, who loves her cruel game,
  Still bent upon some heartless whim,
Shifts her caresses, fickle dame,
  Now kind to me, and now to him:
She stays; 'tis well: but let her shake
  Those wings, her presents I resign,
Cloak me in native worth, and take
  Chaste Poverty undower'd for mine.
Though storms around my vessel rave,
  I will not fall to craven prayers,
Nor bargain by my vows to save
  My Cyprian and Sidonian wares,
Else added to the insatiate main.
  Then through the wild Aegean roar
The breezes and the Brethren Twain
  Shall waft my little boat ashore.

XXX.

EXEGI MONUMENTUM.

And now 'tis done: more durable than brass
  My monument shall be, and raise its head
  O'er royal pyramids: it shall not dread
Corroding rain or angry Boreas,
Nor the long lapse of immemorial time.
  I shall not wholly die: large residue
  Shall 'scape the queen of funerals. Ever new
My after fame shall grow, while pontiffs climb
With silent maids the Capitolian height.
  "Born," men will say, "where Aufidus is loud,
  Where Daunus, scant of streams, beneath him bow'd
The rustic tribes, from dimness he wax'd bright,
First of his race to wed the Aeolian lay
  To notes of Italy." Put glory on,
  My own Melpomene, by genius won,
And crown me of thy grace with Delphic bay.

BOOK IV.

I.

INTERMISSA, VENUS.

Yet again thou wak'st the flame
That long had slumber'd! Spare me, Venus, spare!
   Trust me, I am not the same
As in the reign of Cinara, kind and fair.
   Cease thy softening spells to prove
On this old heart, by fifty years made hard,
   Cruel Mother of sweet Love!
Haste, where gay youth solicits thy regard.
   With thy purple cygnets fly
To Paullus' door, a seasonable guest;
   There within hold revelry,
There light thy flame in that congenial breast.
   He, with birth and beauty graced,
The trembling client's champion, ne'er tongue-tied,
   Master of each manly taste,
Shall bear thy conquering banners far and wide.
   Let him smile in triumph gay,
True heart, victorious over lavish hand,
   By the Alban lake that day
'Neath citron roof all marble shalt thou stand:
   Incense there and fragrant spice
With odorous fumes thy nostrils shall salute;
   Blended notes thine ear entice,
The lyre, the pipe, the Berecyntine flute:
   Graceful youths and maidens bright
Shall twice a day thy tuneful praise resound,
   While their feet, so fair and white,
In Salian measure three times beat the ground.
   I can relish love no more,
Nor flattering hopes that tell me hearts are true,
   Nor the revel's loud uproar,
Nor fresh-wreathed flowerets, bathed in vernal dew.
   Ah! but why, my Ligurine,
Steal trickling tear-drops down my wasted cheek?
   Wherefore halts this tongue of mine,
So eloquent once, so faltering now and weak?
   Now I hold you in my chain,
And clasp you close, all in a nightly dream;
   Now, still dreaming, o'er the plain
I chase you; now, ah cruel! down the stream.

II.

PINDARUM QUISQUIS.

Who fain at Pindar's flight would aim,
  On waxen wings, Iulus, he
Soars heavenward, doom'd to give his name
    To some new sea.
Pindar, like torrent from the steep
  Which, swollen with rain, its banks o'erflows,
With mouth unfathomably deep,
    Foams, thunders, glows,
All worthy of Apollo's bay,
  Whether in dithyrambic roll
Pouring new words he burst away
    Beyond control,
Or gods and god-born heroes tell,
  Whose arm with righteous death could tame
Grim Centaurs, tame Chimaeras fell,
    Out-breathing flame,
Or bid the boxer or the steed
  In deathless pride of victory live,
And dower them with a nobler meed
    Than sculptors give,
Or mourn the bridegroom early torn
  From his young bride, and set on high
Strength, courage, virtue's golden morn,
    Too good to die.
Antonius! yes, the winds blow free,
  When Dirce's swan ascends the skies,
To waft him. I, like Matine bee,
    In act and guise,
That culls its sweets through toilsome hours,
  Am roaming Tibur's banks along,
And fashioning with puny powers
    A laboured song.
Your Muse shall sing in loftier strain
  How Caesar climbs the sacred height,
The fierce Sygambrians in his train,
    With laurel dight,
Than whom the Fates ne'er gave mankind
  A richer treasure or more dear,
Nor shall, though earth again should find
    The golden year.
Your Muse shall tell of public sports,
  And holyday, and votive feast,
For Caesar's sake, and brawling courts
    Where strife has ceased.
Then, if my voice can aught avail,
  Grateful for him our prayers have won,
My song shall echo, "Hail, all hail,
    Auspicious Sun!"

There as you move, "Ho! Triumph, ho!
  Great Triumph!" once and yet again
All Rome shall cry, and spices strow
    Before your train.
Ten bulls, ten kine, your debt discharge:
  A calf new-wean'd from parent cow,
Battening on pastures rich and large,
    Shall quit my vow.
Like moon just dawning on the night
  The crescent honours of his head;
One dapple spot of snowy white,
    The rest all red.

III.

QUEM TU, MELPOMENE.

He whom thou, Melpomene,
Hast welcomed with thy smile, in life arriving,
  Ne'er by boxer's skill shall be
Renown'd abroad, for Isthmian mastery striving;
  Him shall never fiery steed
Draw in Achaean car a conqueror seated;
  Him shall never martial deed
Show, crown'd with bay, after proud kings defeated,
  Climbing Capitolian steep:
But the cool streams that make green Tibur flourish,
  And the tangled forest deep,
On soft Aeolian airs his fame shall nourish.
  Rome, of cities first and best,
Deigns by her sons' according voice to hail me
  Fellow-bard of poets blest,
And faint and fainter envy's growls assail me.
  Goddess, whose Pierian art
The lyre's sweet sounds can modulate and measure,
    Who to dumb fish canst impart
The music of the swan, if such thy pleasure:
    O, 'tis all of thy dear grace
That every finger points me out in going
    Lyrist of the Roman race;
Breath, power to charm, if mine, are thy bestowing!

IV.

QUALEM MINISTRUM.

E'en as the lightning's minister,
  Whom Jove o'er all the feather'd breed
Made sovereign, having proved him sure
  Erewhile on auburn Ganymede;
Stirr'd by warm youth and inborn power,
  He quits the nest with timorous wing,
For winter's storms have ceased to lower,
  And zephyrs of returning spring
Tempt him to launch on unknown skies;
  Next on the fold he stoops downright;
Last on resisting serpents flies,
  Athirst for foray and for flight:
As tender kidling on the grass
  Espies, uplooking from her food,
A lion's whelp, and knows, alas!
  Those new-set teeth shall drink her blood:
So look'd the Raetian mountaineers
  On Drusus:—whence in every field
They learn'd through immemorial years
  The Amazonian axe to wield,
I ask not now: not all of truth
  We seekers find: enough to know
The wisdom of the princely youth
  Has taught our erst victorious foe
What prowess dwells in boyish hearts
  Rear'd in the shrine of a pure home,
What strength Augustus' love imparts
  To Nero's seed, the hope of Rome.
Good sons and brave good sires approve:
  Strong bullocks, fiery colts, attest
Their fathers' worth, nor weakling dove
  Is hatch'd in savage eagle's nest.
But care draws forth the power within,
  And cultured minds are strong for good:
Let manners fail, the plague of sin
  Taints e'en the course of gentle blood.
How great thy debt to Nero's race,
  O Rome, let red Metaurus say,
Slain Hasdrubal, and victory's grace
  First granted on that glorious day
Which chased the clouds, and show'd the sun,
  When Hannibal o'er Italy
Ran, as swift flames o'er pine-woods run,
  Or Eurus o'er Sicilia's sea.
Henceforth, by fortune aiding toil,
  Rome's prowess grew: her fanes, laid waste
By Punic sacrilege and spoil,
  Beheld at length their gods replaced.

Then the false Libyan own'd his doom:—
  "Weak deer, the wolves' predestined prey,
Blindly we rush on foes, from whom
  'Twere triumph won to steal away.
That race which, strong from Ilion's fires,
  Its gods, on Tuscan waters tost,
Its sons, its venerable sires,
  Bore to Ausonia's citied coast;
That race, like oak by axes shorn
  On Algidus with dark leaves rife,
Laughs carnage, havoc, all to scorn,
  And draws new spirit from the knife.
Not the lopp'd Hydra task'd so sore
  Alcides, chafing at the foil:
No pest so fell was born of yore
  From Colchian or from Theban soil.
Plunged in the deep, it mounts to sight
  More splendid: grappled, it will quell
Unbroken powers, and fight a fight
  Whose story widow'd wives shall tell.
No heralds shall my deeds proclaim
  To Carthage now: lost, lost is all:
A nation's hope, a nation's name,
  They died with dying Hasdrubal."
What will not Claudian hands achieve?
  Jove's favour is their guiding star,
And watchful potencies unweave
  For them the tangled paths of war.

V.

DIVIS ORTE BONIS.

Best guardian of Rome's people, dearest boon
  Of a kind Heaven, thou lingerest all too long:
Thou bad'st thy senate look to meet thee soon:
    Do not thy promise wrong.
Restore, dear chief, the light thou tak'st away:
  Ah! when, like spring, that gracious mien of thine
Dawns on thy Rome, more gently glides the day,
    And suns serener shine.
See her whose darling child a long year past
  Has dwelt beyond the wild Carpathian foam;
That long year o'er, the envious southern blast
    Still bars him from his home:
Weeping and praying to the shore she clings,
  Nor ever thence her straining eyesight turns:

So, smit by loyal passion's restless stings,
    Rome for her Caesar yearns.
In safety range the cattle o'er the mead:
   Sweet Peace, soft Plenty, swell the golden grain:
O'er unvex'd seas the sailors blithely speed:
    Fair Honour shrinks from stain:
No guilty lusts the shrine of home defile:
   Cleansed is the hand without, the heart within:
The father's features in his children smile:
    Swift vengeance follows sin.
Who fears the Parthian or the Scythian horde,
   Or the rank growth that German forests yield,
While Caesar lives? who trembles at the sword
    The fierce Iberians wield?
In his own hills each labours down the day,
   Teaching the vine to clasp the widow'd tree:
Then to his cups again, where, feasting gay,
    He hails his god in thee.
A household power, adored with prayers and wine,
   Thou reign'st auspicious o'er his hour of ease:
Thus grateful Greece her Castor made divine,
    And her great Hercules.
Ah! be it thine long holydays to give
   To thy Hesperia! thus, dear chief, we pray
At sober sunrise; thus at mellow eve,
    When ocean hides the day.

VI.

DIVE, QUEM PROLES.

Thou who didst make thy vengeful might
   To Niobe and Tityos known,
And Peleus' son, when Troy's tall height
    Was nigh his own,
Victorious else, for thee no peer,
   Though, strong in his sea-parent's power,
He shook with that tremendous spear
    The Dardan tower.
He, like a pine by axes sped,
   Or cypress sway'd by angry gust,
Fell ruining, and laid his head
    In Trojan dust.
Not his to lie in covert pent
   Of the false steed, and sudden fall
On Priam's ill-starr'd merriment
    In bower and hall:
His ruthless arm in broad bare day

The infant from the breast had torn,
Nay, given to flame, ah, well a way!
    The babe unborn:
But, won by Venus' voice and thine,`
  Relenting Jove Aeneas will'd
With other omens more benign
    New walls to build.
Sweet tuner of the Grecian lyre,
  Whose locks are laved in Xanthus' dews,
Blooming Agyieus! help, inspire
    My Daunian Muse!
'Tis Phoebus, Phoebus gifts my tongue
  With minstrel art and minstrel fires:
Come, noble youths and maidens sprung
    From noble sires,
Blest in your Dian's guardian smile,
  Whose shafts the flying silvans stay,
Come, foot the Lesbian measure, while
    The lyre I play:
Sing of Latona's glorious boy,
  Sing of night's queen with crescent horn,
Who wings the fleeting months with joy,
    And swells the corn.
And happy brides shall say, "'Twas mine,
  When years the cyclic season brought,
To chant the festal hymn divine
    By HORACE taught."

VII.

DIFFUGERE NIVES.

The snow is fled: the trees their leaves put on,
    The fields their green:
Earth owns the change, and rivers lessening run.
    Their banks between.
Naked the Nymphs and Graces in the meads
    The dance essay:
"No 'scaping death" proclaims the year, that speeds
    This sweet spring day.
Frosts yield to zephyrs; Summer drives out Spring,
    To vanish, when
Rich Autumn sheds his fruits; round wheels the ring,—
    Winter again!
Yet the swift moons repair Heaven's detriment:
    We, soon as thrust
Where good Aeneas, Tullus, Ancus went,

What are we? dust.
Can Hope assure you one more day to live
   From powers above?
You rescue from your heir whate'er you give
   The self you love.
When life is o'er, and Minos has rehearsed
   The grand last doom,
Not birth, nor eloquence, nor worth, shall burst
   Torquatus' tomb.
Not Dian's self can chaste Hippolytus
   To life recall,
Nor Theseus free his loved Pirithous
   From Lethe's thrall.

VIII.

DONAREM PATERAS.

Ah Censorinus! to my comrades true
  Rich cups, rare bronzes, gladly would I send:
Choice tripods from Olympia on each friend
  Would I confer, choicer on none than you,
Had but my fate such gems of art bestow'd
  As cunning Scopas or Parrhasius wrought,
  This with the brush, that with the chisel taught
To image now a mortal, now a god.
But these are not my riches: your desire
  Such luxury craves not, and your means disdain:
  A poet's strain you love; a poet's strain
Accept, and learn the value of the lyre.
Not public gravings on a marble base,
  Whence comes a second life to men of might
  E'en in the tomb: not Hannibal's swift flight,
Nor those fierce threats flung back into his face,
Not impious Carthage in its last red blaze,
  In clearer light sets forth his spotless fame,
  Who from crush'd Afric took away—a name,
Than rude Calabria's tributary lays.
Let silence hide the good your hand has wrought.
  Farewell, reward! Had blank oblivion's power
  Dimm'd the bright deeds of Romulus, at this hour,
Despite his sire and mother, he were nought.
Thus Aeacus has 'scaped the Stygian wave,
  By grace of poets and their silver tongue,
  Henceforth to live the happy isles among.
No, trust the Muse: she opes the good man's grave,
And lifts him to the gods. So Hercules,

His labours o'er, sits at the board of Jove:
  So Tyndareus' offspring shine as stars above,
Saving lorn vessels from the yawning seas:
So Bacchus, with the vine-wreath round his hair,
  Gives prosperous issue to his votary's prayer.

IX.

NE FORTE CREDAS.

Think not those strains can e'er expire,
  Which, cradled 'mid the echoing roar
Of Aufidus, to Latium's lyre
  I sing with arts unknown before.
Though Homer fill the foremost throne,
  Yet grave Stesichorus still can please,
And fierce Alcaeus holds his own,
  With Pindar and Simonides.
The songs of Teos are not mute,
  And Sappho's love is breathing still:
She told her secret to the lute,
  And yet its chords with passion thrill.
Not Sparta's queen alone was fired
  By broider'd robe and braided tress,
And all the splendours that attired
  Her lover's guilty loveliness:
Not only Teucer to the field
  His arrows brought, nor Ilion
Beneath a single conqueror reel'd:
  Not Crete's majestic lord alone,
Or Sthenelus, earn'd the Muses' crown:
  Not Hector first for child and wife,
Or brave Deiphobus, laid down
  The burden of a manly life.
Before Atrides men were brave:
  But ah! oblivion, dark and long,
Has lock'd them in a tearless grave,
  For lack of consecrating song.
'Twixt worth and baseness, lapp'd in death,
  What difference? YOU shall ne'er be dumb,
While strains of mine have voice and breath:
  The dull neglect of days to come
Those hard-won honours shall not blight:
  No, Lollius, no: a soul is yours,
Clear-sighted, keen, alike upright
  When fortune smiles, and when she lowers:
To greed and rapine still severe,

Spurning the gain men find so sweet:
A consul, not of one brief year,
  But oft as on the judgment-seat
You bend the expedient to the right,
  Turn haughty eyes from bribes away,
Or bear your banners through the fight,
  Scattering the foeman's firm array.
The lord of boundless revenues,
  Salute not him as happy: no,
Call him the happy, who can use
  The bounty that the gods bestow,
Can bear the load of poverty,
  And tremble not at death, but sin:
No recreant he when called to die
  In cause of country or of kin.

XI.

EST MIHI NONUM.

Here is a cask of Alban, more
  Than nine years old: here grows
Green parsley, Phyllis, and good store
    Of ivy too
  (Wreathed ivy suits your hair, you know)
  The plate shines bright: the altar, strewn
With vervain, hungers for the flow
    Of lambkin's blood.
There's stir among the serving folk;
  They bustle, bustle, boy and girl;
The flickering flames send up the smoke
    In many a curl.
But why, you ask, this special cheer?
  We celebrate the feast of Ides,
Which April's month, to Venus dear,
    In twain divides.
O, 'tis a day for reverence,
  E'en my own birthday scarce so dear,
For my Maecenas counts from thence
    Each added year.
'Tis Telephus that you'd bewitch:
  But he is of a high degree;
Bound to a lady fair and rich,
    He is not free.
O think of Phaethon half burn'd,
  And moderate your passion's greed:
Think how Bellerophon was spurn'd

By his wing'd steed.
So learn to look for partners meet,
  Shun lofty things, nor raise your aims
Above your fortune. Come then, sweet,
    My last of flames
 (For never shall another fair
  Enslave me), learn a tune, to sing
With that dear voice: to music care
    Shall yield its sting.

XII.

JAM VERIS COMITES.

The gales of Thrace, that hush the unquiet sea,
  Spring's comrades, on the bellying canvas blow:
Clogg'd earth and brawling streams alike are free
    From winter's weight of snow.
Wailing her Itys in that sad, sad strain,
  Builds the poor bird, reproach to after time
Of Cecrops' house, for bloody vengeance ta'en
    On foul barbaric crime.
The keepers of fat lambkins chant their loves
  To silvan reeds, all in the grassy lea,
And pleasure Him who tends the flocks and groves
    Of dark-leaved Arcady.
It is a thirsty season, Virgil mine:
  But would you taste the grape's Calenian juice,
Client of noble youths, to earn your wine
    Some nard you must produce.
A tiny box of nard shall bring to light
  The cask that in Sulpician cellar lies:
O, it can give new hopes, so fresh and bright,
    And gladden gloomy eyes.
You take the bait? then come without delay
  And bring your ware: be sure, 'tis not my plan
To let you drain my liquor and not pay,
    As might some wealthy man.
Come, quit those covetous thoughts, those knitted brows,
  Think on the last black embers, while you may,
And be for once unwise. When time allows,
    'Tis sweet the fool to play.

XIII.

AUDIVERE, LYCE.

The gods have heard, the gods have heard my prayer;
  Yes, Lyce! you are growing old, and still
    You struggle to look fair;
      You drink, and dance, and trill
Your songs to youthful Love, in accents weak
  With wine, and age, and passion. Youthful Love!
    He dwells in Chia's cheek,
      And hears her harp-strings move.
Rude boy, he flies like lightning o'er the heath
  Past wither'd trees like you; you're wrinkled now;
    The white has left your teeth
      And settled on your brow.
Your Coan silks, your jewels bright as stars,
  Ah no! they bring not back the days of old,
    In public calendars
      By flying Time enroll'd.
Where now that beauty? where those movements? where
  That colour? what of her, of her is left,
    Who, breathing Love's own air,
      Me of myself bereft,
Who reign'd in Cinara's stead, a fair, fair face,
  Queen of sweet arts? but Fate to Cinara gave
    A life of little space;
      And now she cheats the grave
Of Lyce, spared to raven's length of days,
  That youth may see, with laughter and disgust,
    A fire-brand, once ablaze,
      Now smouldering in grey dust.

XIV.

QUAE CURA PATRUM.

What honours can a grateful Rome,
  A grateful senate, Caesar, give
To make thy worth through days to come
  Emblazon'd on our records live,
Mightiest of chieftains whomsoe'er
  The sun beholds from heaven on high?
They know thee now, thy strength in war,
  Those unsubdued Vindelici.
Thine was the sword that Drusus drew,
  When on the Breunian hordes he fell,
And storm'd the fierce Genaunian crew

E'en in their Alpine citadel,
And paid them back their debt twice told;
  'Twas then the elder Nero came
To conflict, and in ruin roll'd
  Stout Raetian kernes of giant frame.
O, 'twas a gallant sight to see
  The shocks that beat upon the brave
Who chose to perish and be free!
  As south winds scourge the rebel wave
When through rent clouds the Pleiads weep,
  So keen his force to smite, and smite
The foe, or make his charger leap
  Through the red furnace of the fight.
Thus Daunia's ancient river fares,
  Proud Aufidus, with bull-like horn,
When swoln with choler he prepares
  A deluge for the fields of corn.
So Claudius charged and overthrew
  The grim barbarian's mail-clad host,
The foremost and the hindmost slew,
  And conquer'd all, and nothing lost.
The force, the forethought, were thine own,
  Thine own the gods. The selfsame day
When, port and palace open thrown,
  Low at thy footstool Egypt lay,
That selfsame day, three lustres gone,
  Another victory to thine hand
Was given; another field was won
  By grace of Caesar's high command.
Thee Spanish tribes, unused to yield,
  Mede, Indian, Scyth that knows no home,
Acknowledge, sword at once and shield
  Of Italy and queenly Rome.
Ister to thee, and Tanais fleet,
  And Nile that will not tell his birth,
To thee the monstrous seas that beat
  On Britain's coast, the end of earth,
To thee the proud Iberians bow,
  And Gauls, that scorn from death to flee;
The fierce Sygambrian bends his brow,
  And drops his arms to worship thee

XV.

PHOEBUS VOLENTEM.

Of battles fought I fain had told,
  And conquer'd towns, when Phoebus smote
His harp-string: "Sooth, 'twere over-bold
  To tempt wide seas in that frail boat."
Thy age, great Caesar, has restored
  To squalid fields the plenteous grain,
Given back to Rome's almighty Lord
  Our standards, torn from Parthian fane,
Has closed Quirinian Janus' gate,
  Wild passion's erring walk controll'd,
Heal'd the foul plague-spot of the state,
  And brought again the life of old,
Life, by whose healthful power increased
  The glorious name of Latium spread
To where the sun illumes the east
  From where he seeks his western bed.
While Caesar rules, no civil strife
  Shall break our rest, nor violence rude,
Nor rage, that whets the slaughtering knife
  And plunges wretched towns in feud.
The sons of Danube shall not scorn
  The Julian edicts; no, nor they
By Tanais' distant river born,
  Nor Persia, Scythia, or Cathay.
And we on feast and working-tide,
  While Bacchus' bounties freely flow,
Our wives and children at our side,
  First paying Heaven the prayers we owe,
Shall sing of chiefs whose deeds are done,
  As wont our sires, to flute or shell,
And Troy, Anchises, and the son
  Of Venus on our tongues shall dwell.

CARMEN SAECULARE.

PHOEBE, SILVARUMQUE.

Phoebus and Dian, huntress fair,
  To-day and always magnified,
Bright lights of heaven, accord our prayer
    This holy tide,
On which the Sibyl's volume wills
  That youths and maidens without stain
To gods, who love the seven dear hills,
    Should chant the strain!
Sun, that unchanged, yet ever new,
  Lead'st out the day and bring'st it home,

May nought be present to thy view
　　More great than Rome!
Blest Ilithyia! be thou near
　In travail to each Roman dame!
Lucina, Genitalis, hear,
　　Whate'er thy name!
O make our youth to live and grow!
　The fathers' nuptial counsels speed,
Those laws that shall on Rome bestow
　　A plenteous seed!
So when a hundred years and ten
　Bring round the cycle, game and song
Three days, three nights, shall charm again
　　The festal throng.
Ye too, ye Fates, whose righteous doom,
　Declared but once, is sure as heaven,
Link on new blessings, yet to come,
　　To blessings given!
Let Earth, with grain and cattle rife,
　Crown Ceres' brow with wreathen corn;
Soft winds, sweet waters, nurse to life
　　The newly born!
O lay thy shafts, Apollo, by!
　Let suppliant youths obtain thine ear!
Thou Moon, fair "regent of the sky,"
　　Thy maidens hear!
If Rome is yours, if Troy's remains,
　Safe by your conduct, sought and found
Another city, other fanes
　　On Tuscan ground,
For whom, 'mid fires and piles of slain,
　AEneas made a broad highway,
Destined, pure heart, with greater gain.
　　Their loss to pay,
Grant to our sons unblemish'd ways;
　Grant to our sires an age of peace;
Grant to our nation power and praise,
　　And large increase!
See, at your shrine, with victims white,
　Prays Venus and Anchises' heir!
O prompt him still the foe to smite,
　　The fallen to spare!
Now Media dreads our Alban steel,
　Our victories land and ocean o'er;
Scythia and Ind in suppliance kneel,
　　So proud before.
Faith, Honour, ancient Modesty,
　And Peace, and Virtue, spite of scorn,
Come back to earth; and Plenty, see,
　　With teeming horn.

Augur and lord of silver bow,
  Apollo, darling of the Nine,
Who heal'st our frame when languors slow
    Have made it pine;
Lov'st thou thine own Palatial hill,
  Prolong the glorious life of Rome
To other cycles, brightening still
    Through time to come!
From Algidus and Aventine
  List, goddess, to our grave Fifteen!
To praying youths thine ear incline,
    Diana queen!
Thus Jove and all the gods agree!
  So trusting, wend we home again,
Phoebus and Dian's singers we,
    And this our strain.

NOTES.

BOOK I, ODE 3.

THE ESTRANGING MAIN.

"The unplumb'd, salt, estranging sea."
    MATTHEW ARNOLD.

And slow Fate quicken'd Death's once halting pace.

The commentators seem generally to connect Necessitas with Leti; I have preferred to separate them. Necessitas occurs elsewhere in Horace (Book I, Ode 35, v. 17; Book III, Ode 1, v. 14; Ode 24, v. 6) as an independent personage, nearly synonymous with Fate, and I do not see why she should not be represented as accelerating the approach of Death.

BOOK I, ODE 5.

I have ventured to model my version of this Ode, to some extent, on Milton's, "the high-water mark," as it has been termed, "which Horatian translation has attained." I have not, however, sought to imitate his language, feeling that the attempt would be presumptuous in itself, and likely to create a sense of incongruity with the style of the other Odes.

BOOK I, ODE 6.

Who with pared nails encounter youths in fight.

I like Ritter's interpretation of sectis, cut sharp, better than the common one, which supposes the paring of the nails to denote that the attack is not really formidable. Sectis will then be virtually equivalent to Bentley's strictis. Perhaps my translation is not explicit enough.

BOOK I, ODE 7.

And search for wreaths the olive's rifled bower.

Undique decerptam I take, with Bentley, to mean "plucked on all hands," i. e. exhausted as a topic of poetical treatment. He well compares Lucretius, Book I, v. 927—

> "Juvatque novas decerpere flores,
> Insignemque meo capiti petere inde coronam
> Unde prius nulli velarint tempora Musae."

'Tis Teucer leads, 'tis Teucer breathes the wind.

If I have slurred over the Latin, my excuse must be that the precise meaning of the Latin is difficult to catch. Is Teucer called auspex, as taking the auspices, like an augur, or as giving the auspices, like a god? There are objections to both interpretations; a Roman imperator was not called auspex, though he was attended by an auspex, and was said to have the auspicia; auspex is frequently used of one who, as we should say, inaugurates an undertaking, but only if he is a god or a deified mortal. Perhaps Horace himself oscillated between the two meanings; his later commentators do not appear to have distinguished them.

BOOK I, ODE 9.

Since this Ode was printed off, I find that my last stanza bears a suspicious likeness to the version by "C. S. C." I cannot say whether it is a case of mere coincidence, or of unconscious recollection; it certainly is not one of deliberate appropriation. I have only had the opportunity of seeing his book at distant intervals; and now, on finally comparing his translations with my own, I find that, while there are a few resemblances, there are several marked instances of dissimilarity, where, though we have adopted the same metre, we do not approach each other in the least.

BOOK I, ODE 15.

And for your dames divide
On peaceful lyre the several parts of song.

I have taken feminis with divides, but it is quite possible that Orelli may be right in constructing it with grata. The case is really one of those noticed in the Preface, where an interpretation which would not commend itself to a commentator may be adopted by a poetical translator simply as a free rendering.

BOOK I, ODE 27.

Our guest,
Megilla's brother.

There is no warrant in the original for representing this person as a guest of the company; but the Ode is equally applicable to a tavern party, where all share alike, and an entertainment where there is a distinction between hosts and guests.

BOOK I, ODE 28.

I have translated this Ode as it stands, without attempting to decide whether it is dialogue or monologue. Perhaps the opinion which supposes it to be spoken by Horace in his own person, as if he had actually perished in the shipwreck alluded to in Book III, Ode 4, v. 27, "Me… non exstinxit… Sicula Palinurus unda," deserves more attention than it has received.

BOOK II, ODE 1.

Methinks I hear of leaders proud.

Horace supposes himself to hear not the leaders themselves, but Pollio's recitation of their exploits. There is nothing weak in this, as Orelli thinks. Horace has not seen Pollio's work, but compliments him by saying that he can imagine what its finest passages will be like—"I can fancy how you will glow in your description of the great generals, and of Cato." Possibly "Non indecoro pulvere sordidos" may refer to the deaths of the republican generals, whom old recollections would lead Horace to admire. We may then compare Ode 7 of this Book, v. 11—

"Cum fracta virtus, et minaces
Turpe solum tetigere mento,"

where, as will be seen, I agree with Ritter, against Orelli, in supposing death in battle rather than submission to be meant, though Horace, writing from a somewhat different point of view, has chosen there to speak of the vanquished as dying ingloriously.

BOOK II, ODE 3.

Where poplar pale and pine-tree high.

I have translated according to the common reading "Qua pinus … et obliquo," without stopping to inquire whether it is sufficiently supported by MSS. Those who with Orelli prefer "Quo pinus … quid obliquo," may substitute—

Know you why pine and poplar high
  Their hospitable shadows spread
Entwined? why panting waters try
  To hurry down their zigzag bed?

BOOK II, ODE 7.

A man of peace.

Quiritem is generally understood of a citizen with rights undiminished. I have interpreted it of a civilian opposed to a soldier, as in the well-known story in Suetonius (Caes. c. 70), where Julius Caesar takes the tenth legion at their word, and intimates that they are disbanded by the simple substitution of Quirites for milites in his speech to them. But it may very well include both.

BOOK II, ODE 13.

In sacred awe the silent dead
  Attend on each.

"'Sacro digna silentio:' digna eo silentio quod in sacris
faciendis observatur."—RITTER.

BOOK II, ODE 14.

Not though three hundred bullocks flame
   Each year.

I have at last followed Ritter in taking trecenos as loosely put for 365, a steer for each
day in the year. The hyperbole, as he says, would otherwise be too extravagant. And
richer spilth the pavement stain.

"Our vaults have wept
With drunken spilth of wine."
   SHAKESPEARE, Timon of Athens.

BOOK II, ODE 18.

Suns are hurrying suns a-west,
And newborn moons make speed to meet their end.

The thought seems to be that the rapid course of time, hurrying men to the grave,
proves the wisdom of contentment and the folly of avarice. My version formerly did
not express this, and I have altered it accordingly, while I have rendered "Novaeque
pergunt interire lunae" closely, as Horace may perhaps have intended to speak of the
moons as hastening to their graves as men do.

   Yet no hall that wealth e'er plann'd
Waits you more surely than the wider room
   Traced by Death's yet greedier hand.

Fine is the instrumental ablative constructed with destinata, which is itself an ablative
agreeing with aula understood. The rich man looks into the future, and makes
contracts which he may never live to see executed (v. 17—"Tu secanda marmora
Locas sub ipsum funus"); meantime Death, more punctual than any contractor, more
greedy than any encroaching proprietor, has planned with his measuring line a
mansion of a different kind, which will infallibly be ready when the day arrives.

BOOK II, ODE 20.

> I, whom you call
> Your friend, Maecenas.

With Ritter I have rendered according to the interpretation which makes dilecte Maecenas' address to Horace; but it is a choice of evils.

BOOK III, ODE 1.

> And lords of land
> Affect the sea.

Terrae of course goes with fastidiosus, not with dominus. Mine is a loose rendering, not a false interpretation.

BOOK III, ODE 2.

Her robes she keeps unsullied still.

The meaning is not that worth is not disgraced by defeat in contests for worldly honours, but that the honours which belong to worth are such as the worthy never fail to attain, such as bring no disgrace along with them, and such as the popular breath can neither confer nor resume.

> True men and thieves
> Neglected Justice oft confounds.

> "The thieves have bound the true men."
>   SHAKESPEARE, Henry IV, Act ii. Scene 2;
> where see Steevens' note.

BOOK III, ODE 3.

> No more the adulterous guest can charm
> The Spartan queen.

I have followed Ritter in constructing Lacaenae adulterae as a dative with splendet; but I have done so as a poetical translator rather than as a commentator.

BOOK III, ODE 4.

> Or if a graver note than, love,
>   With Phoebus' cittern and his lyre.

I have followed Horace's sense, not his words. I believe, with Ritter, that the alternative is between the pipe as accompanying the vox acuta, and the cithara or lyre as accompanying the vox gravis. Horace has specified the vox acuta, and left the vox gravis to be inferred; I have done just the reverse.

Me, as I lay on Vultur's steep.

In this and the two following stanzas I have paraphrased Horace, with a view to bring out what appears to be his sense. There is, I think, a peculiar force in the word fabulosae, standing as it does at the very opening of the stanza, in close connection with me, and thus bearing the weight of all the intervening words till the very end, where its noun, palumbes, is introduced at last. Horace says in effect, "I, too, like other poets, have a legend of my infancy." Accordingly I have thrown the gossip of the country-side into the form of an actual speech. Whether I am justified in heightening the marvellous by making the stock-doves actually crown the child, instead of merely laying branches upon him, I am not so sure; but something more seems to be meant than the covering of leaves, which the Children in the Wood, in our own legend, receive from the robin.

> Loves the leafy growth
> Of Lycia next his native wood.

Some of my predecessors seem hardly to distinguish between the Lyciae dumeta and the natalem silvam of Delos, Apollo's attachment to both of which warrants the two titles Delius et Patareus. I knew no better way of marking the distinction within the compass of a line and a half than by making Apollo exhibit a preference where Horace speaks of his likings as co-ordinate.

Strength mix'd with mind is made more strong.

"Mixed" is not meant as a precise translation of temperatam, chastened or restrained, though "to mix" happens to be one of the shades of meaning of temperare.

BOOK III, ODE 5.

The fields we spoil'd with corn are green.

The later editors are right in not taking Marte nostro with coli as well as with populata. As has been remarked to me, the pride of the Roman is far more forcibly expressed by the complaint that the enemy have been able to cultivate fields that Rome has ravaged than by the statement that Roman captives have been employed to cultivate the fields they had ravaged as invaders. The latter proposition, it is true, includes the former; but the new matter draws off attention from the old, and so weakens it.

Who once to faithless foes has knelt.

"Knelt" is not strictly accurate, expressing Bentley's dedidit rather than the common, and doubtless correct, text, credidit.

> And, girt by friends that mourn'd him, sped
>   * * *
> The press of kin he push'd apart.

I had originally reversed amicos and propinquos, supposing it to be indifferent which of them was used in either stanza. But a friend has pointed out to me that a distinction is probably intended between the friends who attended Regulus and the kinsmen who sought to prevent his going.

BOOK III, ODE 8.

Lay down that load of state-concern.

I have translated generally; but Horace's meaning is special, referring to Maecenas' office of prefect of the city.

BOOK III, ODE 9.

Buttmann complains of the editors for specifying the interlocutors as Horace and Lydia, which he thinks as incongruous as if in an English amoebean ode Collins were to appear side by side with Phyllis. The remark may be just as affects the Latin, though Ode 19 of the present Book, and Odes 33 and 36 of Book I, might be adduced to show that Horace does not object to mixing Latin and Greek names in the same poem; but it does not apply to a translation, where to the English reader's apprehension Horace and Lydia will seem equally real, equally fanciful.

BOOK III, ODE 17.

Lamia was doubtless vain of his pedigree; Horace accordingly banters him good-humouredly by spending two stanzas out of four in giving him his proper ancestral designation. To shorten the address by leaving out a stanza, as some critics and some translators have done, is simply to rob Horace's trifle of its point.

BOOK III, ODE 23.

There is something harsh in the expression of the fourth stanza of this Ode in the Latin. Tentare cannot stand without an object, and to connect it, as the commentators do, with deos is awkward. I was going to remark that possibly some future Bentley would conjecture certare, or litare, when I found that certare had been anticipated by Peerlkamp, who, if not a Bentley, was a Bentleian. But it would not be easy to account for the corruption, as the fact that the previous line begins with cervice would rather have led to the change of tentare into certare than vice versa.

BOOK III, ODE 24.

> Let Necessity but drive
> Her wedge of adamant into that proud head.

I have translated this difficult passage nearly as it stands, not professing to decide whether tops of buildings or human heads are meant. Either is strange till explained; neither seems at present to be supported by any exact parallel in ancient literature or ancient art. Necessity with her nails has met us before in Ode 35 of Book I, and Orelli describes an Etruscan work of art where she is represented with that cognizance; but though the nail is an appropriate emblem of fixity, we are apparently not told where it is to be driven. The difficulty here is further complicated by the following metaphor of the noose, which seems to be a new and inconsistent image.

BOOK III, ODE 29.

Nor gaze on Tibur, never dried.

With Ritter I have connected semper udum (an interpretation first suggested by Tate, who turned ne into ut); but I do not press it as the best explanation of the Latin. The general effect of the stanza is the same either way.

Those piles, among the clouds at home.

I have understood molem generally of the buildings of Rome, not specially of Maecenas' tower. The parallel passage in Virg. Aen. i. 421—

> "Miratur molem Aeneas, magalia quondam,
> Miratur portas strepitumque et strata viarum"—

is in favour of the former view.

What once the flying hour has brought.

I have followed Ritter doubtfully. Compare Virg. Georg. i. 461,—

"Quid vesper serus vehat."

Shall waft my little boat ashore.

I have hardly brought out the sense of the Latin with sufficient clearness. Horace says that if adversity comes upon him he shall accept it, and be thankful for what is left him, like a trader in a tempest, who, instead of wasting time in useless prayers for the safety of his goods, takes at once to the boat and preserves his life.

BOOK IV, ODE 2.

> And spices straw
> Before your train.

I had written "And gifts bestow at every fane;" but Ritter is doubtless right in explaining dabimus tura of the burning of incense in the streets during the procession. About the early part of the stanza I am less confident; but the explanation which makes Antonius take part in the procession as praetor, the reading adopted being Tuque dum procedis, is perhaps the least of evils.

BOOK IV, ODE 3.

On soft AEolian airs his fame shall nourish.

Horace evidently means that the scenery of Tibur contributes to the formation of lyric genius. It is Wordsworth's doctrine in the germ; though, if the author had been asked what it involved, perhaps he would not have gone further than Ritter, who resolves it all into the conduciveness of a pleasant retreat to successful composition.

BOOK IV, ODE 4.

I have deranged the symmetry of the two opening similes, making the eagle the subject of the sentence in the first, the kid in the second, an awkwardness which the Latin is able to avoid by its power of distinguishing cases by inflexion. I trust, however, that it will not offend an English reader.

> Whence in every field
> They learned.

Horace seems to allude jokingly to some unseasonable inquiry into the antiquity of the armour of these Alpine tribes, which had perhaps been started by some less skilful celebrator of the victory; at the same time that he gratifies his love of lyrical commonplace by a parenthetical digression in the style of Pindar.

> And watchful potencies unweave
>   For them the tangled paths of war.

On the whole, Ritter seems right, after Acron, in understanding curae sagaces of the counsels of Augustus, whom Horace compliments similarly in the Fourteenth Ode of this Book, as the real author of his step- son's victories. He is certainly right in giving the stanza to Horace, not to Hannibal. Even a courtly or patriotic Roman would have shrunk from the bad taste of making the great historical enemy of Italy conclude his lamentation over his own and his country's deep sorrow by a flattering prophecy of the greatness of his antagonist's family.

BOOK IV, ODE 9.

> 'Twixt worth and baseness, lapp'd in death,
>   What difference?

I believe I have expressed Horace's meaning, though he has chosen to express himself as if the two things compared were dead worthlessness and uncelebrated worth. By fixing the epithet sepultae to inertiae he doubtless meant to express that the natural and appropriate fate of worthlessness was to be dead, buried, and forgotten. But the context shows that he was thinking of the effect of death and its consequent oblivion on worth and worthlessness alike, and contending that the poet alone could remedy the undiscriminating and unjust award of destiny. Throughout the first half of the Ode, however, Horace has rather failed to mark the transitions of thought. He begins by assuring himself and, by implication, those whom he celebrates, of immortality, on the ground that the greatest poets are not the only poets; he then exchanges this thought for another, doubtless suggested by it, that the heroes of poetry are not the only heroes, though the very fact that there have been uncelebrated heroes is used to show that celebration by a poet is everything.

> Or bear your banners through the fight,
>   Scattering the Joemari's firm array.

It seems, on the whole, simpler to understand this of actual victories obtained by Lollius as a commander, than of moral victories obtained by him as a judge. There is harshness in passing abruptly from the judgment-seat to the battle-field; but to speak of the judgment-seat as itself the battle-field would, I think, be harsher still.

FINIS.

Made in the USA
San Bernardino, CA
22 January 2016